How to Develop a Team Ministry and Make It Work

How to Develop a Team Ministry and Make It Work

Ervin F. Henkelmann
Stephen J. Carter

Publishing House
St. Louis

The quotation on pp. 37—38 is from pp. 97—99 of *Life Together* by Dietrich Bonhoeffer, translated by John W. Doberstein. Copyright 1954 by Harper & Row, Publishers, Inc. Used by permission of the publisher.

Scripture quotations are from The Holy Bible: NEW INTERNATIONAL VERSION, © 1978 by the International Bible Society. Used by permission of Zondervan Bible Publishers.

Copyright © 1985 by Concordia Publishing House,
3558 South Jefferson Avenue, St. Louis, MO 63118-3968.
Manufactured in the United States of America.

Library of Congress Cataloging in Publication Data

Henkelmann, Ervin F., 1938-
        How to develop a team ministry and make it work.

        1.   Group ministry.   I.   Carter, Stephen J., 1941-
I.   Title.
V675.H46   1985   253   84-15625
ISBN   0-570-03946-0 (pbk.)

---

1 2 3 4 5 6 7 8 9 10   MAL   94 93 92 91 90 89 88 87 86 85

Contents

6

Introduction

PROFESSIONAL TEAM MINISTRY! That's what this book is all about—how to develop a team ministry and make it work! We sense an urgency to improve team relationships among professional staff in the local parish so that God can work through us to carry out Christ's Great Commission more effectively. Team ministry takes time to build. Effective team ministry also makes better use of the time God has given us to equip His people for the work of ministry. Now is a good time to examine your team ministry and to seek ways to bring it in line with God's plan for your parish.

You may be a senior pastor looking for better ways to relate to that assistant pastor, vicar/intern, director of Christian education, or school principal. You may desire a greater closeness and more productive ministry with your team but are not certain how to achieve it. Perhaps you feel too remote or directive in your approach and would like to get more feedback and support from your staff. Or perhaps you picture yourself as too much the "nice person," well-liked but not very certain of your direction or leadership. You are seeking help on how to make possible a balanced team ministry that combines effective leadership with harmonious team relationships.

You may be a disgruntled director of Christian education. You want to serve the Lord as part of the team. You are willing to let the pastor serve as overall shepherd of the flock, but you want the necessary authority to lead the congregation in your area of special training. You are not sure how the congregation understands or accepts your role, and you do not always feel supported by the pastor. You have attempted to talk things out with him, but you can't see any improvement in your relationship. You wonder if this book might help you understand your situation better and suggest practical ways to strengthen your ministry and team relationships.

You may be a principal caught in the middle between pastor and faculty. You basically know that your task is to provide Christ-centered education for the children of the school. You want the faculty to work together effectively to accomplish that goal, but you sometimes find your hands tied. The pastor doesn't seem to understand the unique needs of your staff and is demanding more performance from them. He expects you to put the pressure on them for more service in other areas of the parish. He also insists on some curriculum changes that do not seem to be in the best interests of the school. On the other hand, some of your faculty members do have a narrow concept of their ministry. They seem to want only what is convenient for their classroom work. They want you to complain to the board of education. You are hoping that this book will help you improve lines of communication and foster better relationships between pastor and school staff.

You may be a lay leader in your local parish. You are aware that professional staff members are experiencing serious conflict or that they seem to work independently without much communication. Other lay members have talked to you about problems in staff relationships. You wonder how you can approach the problem. You hope this book will help you understand the role of lay leaders in promoting and building good team relationships among professional staff in your parish.

Your unique team ministry needs and questions will vary greatly with circumstance and personnel. But your interest in serving effectively and cooperatively impels you to read on. Ignoring problems or sweeping them under the rug won't work. Postponing action on team relationships will only intensify the problems. For the sake of the Gospel and the mission of the church, now is a good time to rethink your team ministry.

Time for Mission

Team ministry concerns do not exist in isolation. Your personal problems and concerns, though valid, do not in themselves justify a book on team ministry. Team ministry exists for mission. Jesus Christ commands us, "Go and make disciples of all nations, baptizing them in the name of the Father and of the Son and of the Holy Spirit" (Matt. 28:19). He founded the church, His body, as a missionary arm to share His Gospel with the world. He provides the powerful Word and Sacraments to call us into His body and to nourish us for outreach to a sinful world. The early church in the Book of Acts met together for worship and fellowship and scattered to spread the Good News of God's love in Jesus Christ, crucified and risen. God provides the office of the public ministry to equip the saints for this Gospel mission to the world. Team ministry, then, in the local parish exists for the church's mission.

Now is a good time for more effective team ministry because the mission challenges and opportunities are unparalleled. Billions need to hear about Jesus Christ as Savior. The worldwide challenge has an impact on the cities, towns, and rural parishes of North America. Multi-ethnic groups are present in many areas. People are confused and troubled, traumatized by rapid change, fearful of nuclear holocaust, numbed and alienated by family breakdown, purposeless and empty in their lives. They need a relationship with God through Christ and a fellowship with His body, the church. The mission calls for human and financial resources to be effectively organized to provide word and deed Gospel-sharing and ongoing discipleship.

The great mission challenge requires effective professional team ministry in local parishes to mobilize God's people for caring ministry. When team members fight with each other or go in separate directions, huge amounts of energy are wasted, and our Gospel mission is impaired. The stakes are high. Effective and harmonious team ministry, in which the staff glorifies God and reaches out with the Gospel, results in a mission-minded church that accepts today's mission challenge. Now is a good time for team ministry because it's time for mission.

Time for Reflection

Now is a good time also for reflection. What insights for team ministry can we gain by looking at the world and the church today? Where do our particular questions and problems fit into the total picture? How is the need for team ministry substantiated by a look at the world and the church?

Reflection on a Plus and Minus World

We can learn much that is positive from the way the world accomplishes challenging goals through teamwork. The space program, especially the Apollo moon project, demonstrated what could be accomplished by combining modern technology with careful planning and coordinated human resources. The ailing Chrysler corporation made a dramatic comeback by forging new partnerships between management and labor, government and private sources. Dramatic new breakthroughs are occurring constantly in a computer technology that links people together in a teamwork setting. Teleconferencing and interactive video enable people in industry or education to work together more closely.

In management circles recent emphasis has been placed on a systems approach, which would help workers to see themselves as part of the whole. Leaders take great pains to discover how the whole effort can be coordinated for effective results. In Japan quality circles provide for participation throughout an industrial plant in decision making and problem solving. We are urged to have clear goals, to understand our roles, and to support one another in the common effort. The world of administration also has offered practical help for effective ministry in the area of time management. Reflection on today's world certainly provides some pluses for team ministry.

However, today's world also presents some distinct minuses. So many people are absorbed with themselves to the exclusion of involvement with others. Many overemphasize self-improvement through health, physical fitness, positive thinking, assertiveness training, private meditation, and a host of other personal growth items. People live alone, isolate themselves in front of the television when others are present, play video games by the hour, and shun commitments to relationships or organizations. They stress competition rather than cooperation. Many seek religious satisfaction from the electronic church, where they can be entertained and have their needs satisfied without any responsibility to a local parish or any need for interpersonal relationships.

Families are breaking down at an alarming rate. Rather than viewing themselves as part of a God-ordained unit of society that works as a team, family members seek their own satisfaction, create high expectations of other family members, and simply leave to seek other relationships when things don't work out. Very little closeness or intimacy is experienced within many families. These minuses in modern society can be traced to the root sin of selfishness and pride, which separates human beings from God and each other.

Both the pluses and the minuses of our world make a strong case for consideration of team ministry in the local parish. When we see government, business, and industry working together as a team to accomplish significant goals, we recognize the potential for more effective team ministry as we share the Gospel. Technology and management strategies can be properly used as gifts of God's creation.

When we view the selfish, private, and highly competitive society in which we live, we realize how desperately our world needs to see the fellowship of God's people at work to share Jesus Christ in word and deed. We recognize the sharp contrast between church and world. And we desire to let God build our professional team ministry relationships so that we can model a Christ-centered, Spirit-led, person-oriented ministry to the church and world.

Reflection on a Plus and Minus Church

On the one hand, today's church, led by God's Spirit working through the Word, gives evidence of some marvelous pluses for team ministry. Many Christians have caught the mission vision. They rejoice in the opportunity to worship, study the Word, witness of the Savior, and serve together in caring ways. They accept themselves as stewards of God. They are discovering their God-given gifts and are using them to build up the body of Christ. The laity is awakening to God's calling for their lives.

Church bodies are accepting their responsibility to exercise leadership in sound Scriptural doctrine, mission outreach, and Christian fellowship. They provide training for pastors and other church professionals with a mission emphasis. They encourage Gospel renewal in the local parishes.

Some local parishes are also catching the Scriptural strategy for mission. They are growing in spiritual depth and in outreach. They train lay leaders. And they provide the necessary professional staff. These pluses within the church provide impetus for a book on professional team ministry because effective and harmonious team relationships fit beautifully into a New Testament ministry.

At the same time, all is not well within the church. Satan works overtime to keep churches ineffective. Some churches merely exist for survival. They maintain the status quo. They form social clubs of familiar members and resent outside intrusions. They do not relate to their larger church body or to the mission challenge in the world.

Churches, once close-knit, are also experiencing some new problems. Ethnic churches are breaking down. Members come from diverse social, ethnic, and religious backgrounds. The common church heritage gets lost as new members are assimilated. Family problems in society also affect the church. Personal and family troubles become more complicated. The sense of community or fellowship lessens. More ministry is needed to meet these new problems. More organization also appears essential.

Church problems, the result of sin, are further aggravated by many professional team ministries in trouble. Personalities clash. Congregations line up behind different staff members. Conflicts surface. Pride rears its ugly head. Backbiting occurs. Staff members are demotivated and discouraged. Ministries lag. Staff members work in separate directions, sometimes canceling each other out. Sometimes poor team ministry ruins the congregation. Sometimes an intransigent and apathetic parish discourages and divides a team ministry.

Minuses in the church underscore the need for effective team ministry. Team members need to drink in the Gospel, persistently communicate and pursue Biblical goals, and model Christ-centered, caring relationships. Now is a good time for reflection on a professional team ministry in the light of a plus and minus world and church.

Time to Team

We take the position that now is the time to team. Good use of time to build team ministry will bring a rich harvest of mission.

We suggest, first of all, that you take time to imagine what the team could one day be like. If you work at visualizing what God intends your team to be, He can lead you toward that goal. You will want clear expectations, a solid spiritual foundation, harmonious relationships, and effective ministry. Great blessings will flow from an ideal picture with which lay and professional leaders can agree.

You will next need time to practice responsible and accountable leadership. Every parish has to wrestle with the leadership questions: Who leads? What makes a leader ? How does one lead? The answers to those questions should help you come to grips with the unique leadership blend in your church staff.

You will also consider the starting time for team ministry. Obviously, readers preparing to begin a team ministry will profit from this discussion, but so will those who are experiencing staff changes or taking a position in another church. Every team can reflect on how well the staff is blended and bonded. You will learn the importance of knowledge, skills, habits, and attitudes in blending as a staff. You can rate your team ministry quotient. You can briefly consider how to become familiar with staff candidates and how to orient new staff members.

You will learn the importance of taking time to know yourself and your role. Even if you are struggling currently in a team ministry situation, you will see how to accept yourself as God's child and servant and how to identify your unique gifts in the body of Christ. Knowing yourself and your relationships to the other team members will help you to serve more joyfully and effectively.

Knowing yourself better will lead you naturally to see the importance of putting time into improving relationships. You will learn to maximize all staff contact times. You will both plan and spontaneously discover the relationship payoffs of a caring staff. You will see the value of forgiveness in a staff setting and consider the potential of an annual staff retreat.

Finally, you will discover ways of using time effectively to get the job done. Harmonious relationships need to be complemented with effective ministry. Considering the other staff members as you prepare, making joint use of the secretarial staff, and establishing mutual deadlines will make you more effective. Investigating the purposes for meetings and time-effective meeting procedures will strengthen your team ministry. Considering the building and equipment in terms of professional team ministry can also help both your relationships and your effectiveness.

Are you ready to take the plunge into team ministry reflection? The water is just right. If you are just learning to swim or struggling with a weight around your neck, the pool may seem dangerously deep in spots. But the depths are marked along the way. You can go as deep as you would like. Some items may be reserved for a later swim. This book may be a springboard to a new experience for you. You may find the water more to your liking. We haven't even talked about the lifeguard who stands always ready and alert to rescue, encourage, and sustain you. So why not dive in? Now is a good time!

1
Time to Imagine What the Team Could Be Like

YOU'RE OFF TO A GOOD START. Team members, long awaited, are all in place. The congregation is ready for your ministry. Much work beckons. You're off to a good start.

Or are you? You may be assuming that it's time for action by the team, time to get busy in ministry, time to go separate ways and fulfill your individual dreams for the parish. But are you willing to take time to imagine what the team could one day be like? Imagine God's plan for your parish, for your team, for you. Let your imagination soar. Talk it over. Jot down notes on paper. Ask lay leaders what they imagine for your church and for your ministry. Taking time to develop a picture of your team functioning as God intends in your parish will produce very helpful, practical, and fruitful results for the future.

The harsh realities will settle in soon enough. Friction, misunderstandings, poor communication, failures, road blocks, frustration, discouragement, and disillusionment will rear their ugly heads and attempt to derail you from your mission and your team relationships. In short, sin and selfishness will disrupt your good intentions. But if you have taken the time to imagine what the team could one day be like, and if you hold that vision regularly before you, God can help you to confess your failures, receive His forgiveness, address your problems, and become more and more the kind of team He wants you to be. This chapter is designed to help you arrive at a vision of your team's dynamic potential in the parish where God has placed you.

Clear Expectations

So often, team members and parish leaders are not clear as to what the team is trying to accomplish and how it is to function. A growing parish with one pastor will decide that the pastor is overworked and needs additional staff help. The members may realize that their church will not be able to continue growing without additional staff. With great enthusiasm but without much planning, they call a second professional worker—a second pastor, a director of Christian education, or a lay worker.

A vague written description plus conversation with the called staff person attempts to articulate the expectations for team ministry. The new worker has his own impressions and expectations that may lead him to accept the call. The pastor, feeling overburdened, looks forward to relief from his many duties and to letting the new staff member handle some areas that he did not particularly enjoy. He wants to share the ministry and let the new team member gain acceptance in the parish. At the same time, he has become accustomed to leadership and wants to maintain visible recognition as the leader. The lay leaders also have expectations for the team that may or may not be stated. They probably will hold the head pastor accountable for the new staff member whether or not the team members have this understanding. More will be shared about the issue of responsible and accountable leadership in the next chapter. Both professional and lay leaders may fail to relate the new team ministry to a clear view of the mission and goals of the parish. Fuzzy expectations will lead to a frustrating team ministry and an unfulfilled parish mission.

The ideal team ministry will regularly clarify expectations. In-depth study of God's Word by professional staff and laity will reveal God's intentions for His church in the world with the Gospel as the power for that ministry. The team will both guide and respond to the growing parish understanding of their mission in their community and the world. The individual team members will communicate their expectations based on parish needs, individual strengths and weaknesses, and their willingness to serve God and others.

Clear expectations need to be expressed on paper in the form of job descriptions. Linked to parish goals, they can express both the normal responsibilities of each staff member and the relationships between staff members and lay leaders. Appendix A contains some sample job descriptions. Job descriptions can be profitably written for all staff members—pastors, directors of Christian education, deaconesses, youth workers, lay assistants, principals, teachers, secretaries, and custodians. Job descriptions are initially prepared when a worker joins the staff, but they should be reviewed and revised on a regular basis as the team blends together. Each team member should have input into the review of the job description.

Mutually accepted job descriptions are essential for good communication between professional and lay leaders. They are intended to encourage a good flow of communication so that the roles and relationships between staff members can be continually clarified. Every team is constantly in the process of finding the most effective way of ministering together. The goals and needs of the parish, the discovery of gifts and talents, and the motivation of the workers will determine the changing roles and relationships between staff members.

The team members are willing to spend time sharing their dreams for the parish and for their own ministries. Their expectations may conflict between what is desired and what is possible or what is good for the parish and what is good for the worker. However, the process of discussing those expectations will open up new possibilities and new ways of involving lay and professional staff in a common parish mission. Through this process what is written on paper will accurately describe parish expectations, and motivated team members will live up to what is on paper.

Expectations also include the care of team members in such important areas as salary, housing, continuing education, vacations, and regular time off. The lay leadership of the parish has the responsibility for developing policies regarding these matters that are achievable, equitable, consistent, and acceptable to team members. A personnel committee can be quite helpful in bringing together concerned lay leaders who have responsibility for professional staff. Often a board of elders and a board of education make independent decisions about provision for workers that cause friction and misunderstanding. The personnel committee can provide a forum for discussion of team care. Team members should be consulted as to their needs and hopes, and all proposals and decisions should be clearly communicated in order to avoid misunderstandings.

Professional and lay leaders together can develop a handbook of personnel policies that cover most of the expectations regarding staff care and performance. These policies can anticipate areas of recurring concern and handle them in writing. The policies are open to annual review and revision with input from laity and professional staff, but they provide a basis for clear expectations and ongoing discussion. Appendix B contains a sample table of contents for a congregation's personnel handbook.

Clear expectations, therefore, about the parish's purpose and its team ministry provide the first ingredient for an ideal team situation. It's worth taking time to visualize your team having clear expectations in every area. Unlike the blind men who described the same elephant in totally different ways depending on whether they were touching the trunk, the tusks, the ears, or the head, your team gets the whole parish picture through careful, caring, ongoing, Biblical, Christ-centered discussion of God's plan for your parish and your staff. Laity and professional staff join together in this important activity of clarifying expectations.

Solid Spiritual Foundation

Many team ministries in local churches fail to work. Initial enthusiasm quickly fades. Dissension sets in. Each staff member goes in a separate direction. Team meetings are regarded as a necessary evil to be endured. One or more staff members finally leave, looking for greener pastures and a more satisfying team ministry elsewhere. Sometimes team arrangements seem to work better in industry or business than in the church of Jesus Christ. Why? What causes deterioration of staff relationships and effective ministry in a church or church/school setting? While this entire book addresses itself to these questions, the present section asks you to visualize for your team the importance of a solid spiritual foundation, which can empower you for harmonious relationships and effective ministry.

God has given us the glorious Gospel of His Son Jesus Christ. Lost in sin, we flounder hopelessly in selfishness, greed, confusion, and despair. We stand guilty before God on the basis of our puny merits. But God in His mercy sent His Son Jesus to live a perfect life in our stead, to die on the cross in full payment for our sins, and to rise from the grave on the third day as proof of His victory over sin, death, and Satan. God declares us righteous in His sight on the basis of Christ's death and resurrection. By His grace alone we are brought to faith and incorporated into the family of God through our baptism in the name of the Triune God. Justified by God's grace for Christ's sake through faith, we lead lives of service to God and others by the power of the Holy Spirit working through God's Word and the sacraments of Holy Baptism and Holy Communion. God alone brings team ministry into being, directs the team in His service to the world, and sustains the team in times of trial and problems.

This Gospel is well known to workers in the pastoral and teaching ministries of the church. This Gospel has changed our lives, brought us into some aspect of full-time service, and provided the message for our ministry in word and deed. Individually, we believe the Gospel. Corporately, we receive that Gospel through regularly receiving the Word and Sacraments in worship.

Yet in our team ministry relationships how often the Gospel is neglected. We meet for business—God's business, to be sure. We discuss relationship problems, at least occasionally. We get together for social purposes. We may even grace our meetings with a brief devotion. Nevertheless, we often do not permit the Gospel to be central in our team. As a result, when problems and tensions arise, the team is unable to cope or to respond in a Gospel manner.

Picture for yourself a team ministry with a solid spiritual foundation. In what ways would God be present with His enabling love? How would you be growing individually and as a team? How would this foundation affect your respective ministries?

First, each team member would be experiencing a rich personal devotional life. In addition to formal study and preparation for worship, preaching, teaching, and other ministry, the individual would be regularly reading Scripture, Christian doctrinal classics, and devotional literature for personal strength and edification. Prayer would be a vital part of this personal devotional life as individual needs, parish needs, and the well-being of the church-at-large are constantly in focus. Confession of sins, praise, and thanksgiving would flow from the regular time spent with the Word of God. Imagine what each team member could bring to the team relationships on the basis of God's Gospel freely bestowed in the personal devotional life.

Second, the team would participate regularly and enthusiastically in the corporate worship and Christian growth opportunities of the parish. What a growing joy to gather with the people of God to hear the Word, receive the sacrament of Holy Communion, sing God's praises, and study the Word in various settings. God builds a solid spiritual foundation not only in the parish as a whole but also in the team members through these parish activities. The staff can share the meaning of corporate worship and Bible study.

Third, the team members grow spiritually through the Gospel ministry that they carry out alongside God's people in the parish. Visiting the unchurched, calling on inactive members, counseling the troubled, comforting the sick, dying, and bereaved, teaching children and adults, working with youth and adults in groups, boards, and committees—all of these activities provide opportunities for using the Gospel message, relying on it, and receiving it from others. A Gospel ministry itself builds a spiritual foundation in the proclaimer. In that sense, rich Gospel worship, preaching, and teaching and an active Gospel outreach in the parish and community provide a strong support for the professional team that is also encouraging that ministry.

Finally, the Gospel needs to find a central place in the actual meetings and interactions of your team. Regular team Bible study would be a necessity. You could study together the appointed lessons for the week, a book of the Bible, or an appropriate topic for the parish situation at hand. The Bible study would stress not so much formal theological study or argumentation as personal sharing on the basis of the Word. Effective team Bible study would provide an atmosphere for confronting relationship problems, confessing personal sins and shortcomings, raising personal and professional needs, and discussing Gospel ministry priorities for the parish. The Word would be central, and all participants would place themselves under that Word in the context of their needs. Special times could also be set aside for in-depth study of Scripture and Christian doctrine in addition to these regular Bible sharing times.

Prayer is another essential ingredient of your team meetings and interactions. Regular praise and thanksgiving from liturgical and nonliturgical sources can be used by God to fill your team with an awareness of a caring Triune God and His gracious actions in the world, including your parish, your team, and your individual lives. The routine and sometimes volatile nature of team discussions can be more joyfully faced in the context of praise to God.

Prayer together also should include supplication for the many needs of the team members and their families, the members of the parish, the un-churched, parish needs and problems, the church-at-large, the nation, and the world. The concerns are many. You might want to consider a prayer list that would provide an opportunity for systematic reflection on God's actions in the lives of His people. Regular, personal prayer in your team meetings can do much to bring your team together in the Gospel and focus on God's provision. The honesty and caring of your prayer life together will grow as God builds a stronger spiritual foundation in your lives.

Sharing your Gospel ministry in the team meetings provides another source of strength. Each team member works in a unique section of the parish. Every day God works His Gospel miracles in the lives of people and groups in the parish and beyond. Sometimes He works quietly and simply, at other times more dramatically. To the extent that the team members are willing to share the joys of ministry, the whole team is strengthened and focused on a Gospel ministry. The personal sharing includes also burdens and problems, because in the team interaction God's purposes and actions often become clear for the burdened team member. Spiritual maturity is needed for such sharing so that jealousy or fear of reprisal does not restrict the sharing and make it wooden and mechanical.

We hope you can see the need for a solid spiritual foundation in your team. Satan will work overtime to restrict your use of the Gospel, to focus your attention on problems and divisions rather than on God's power at work in your team and parish. The devotional life takes discipline and determination individually and as a team. The flesh will contend with the spirit within you. It will be tough to set and follow schedules and to stick to agreed-upon time allotments. But the benefits for the team ministry relationship and effective ministry in the parish will be enormous as you permit God to build within your ministry team a solid spiritual foundation based on Bible study, prayer, and Gospel sharing together. This will pave the way for more harmonious relationships in your team.

Harmonious Relationships

Imagine what your team could one day be like. Take the time. You will have clear expectations about your own role, your team, and God's plan for your parish. You will be letting God build a solid spiritual foundation for your team. Consequently you will also be experiencing harmonious relationships within the team.

A large midwestern parish is a good example of rebuilding through harmonious relationships. The two previous pastors had been seriously divided. They scarcely spoke to each other. Congregational members lined up behind one or the other. Both claimed to be representing God's directions for the parish. The large parish school seemed to be separate from the church. The principal and teachers went their own way, trying to avoid getting involved in the conflict between the pastors. Their priorities were to create the best working conditions for the school without considering the mission of the parish. Each teacher considered his or her classroom a little kingdom in its own right. Faculty meetings were tolerated as a necessary evil for business purposes. The members, aware of the problems within the professional staff, saw no direction and were affected by the disharmony.

Both pastors move elsewhere, and a new man accepts the call as the senior pastor. He comes to lead by serving and listening. He makes it a point to get acquainted with each staff member. Gradually he seeks to gain the confidence of the principal and teachers. Convinced of God's directions for the parish, he nevertheless joins in a study of Scripture with the staff. Together they explore God's Word. Each staff member is encouraged to share his or her values and opinions. Each is affirmed as a unique servant of God with special talents to be used in the Lord's service in the parish. The head pastor models a style of listening, caring, affirming, and valuing the contributions of each staff member. The staff responds to his leadership.

The staff grows more united around a common purpose for the parish. The school is seen as a part of the total ministry. Parish problems are faced together. Staff members begin to encourage one another and pitch in to help. One-on-one and group relationships are open. Staff members disagree at times and have the courage to confront each other in love when needed. But the confrontations occur because of a mutual trust and dependence on God's love in Christ. Staff meetings include times for confessing shortcomings and asking forgiveness.

The congregation begins to notice the new spirit among staff members. They hear teachers speaking highly of the pastoral ministry and the pastor pointing out to them the Christian dedication and talents of the teaching staff. A second pastor is called to complement the team ministry. He likewise is accepted as a gifted servant of the Word and respected for his contributions. The common parish purpose is shared, and he is encouraged to find his unique place in the team relationships. Both pastors agree to meet regularly for Bible study and sharing. They agree to disagree with each other in private discussion but to work out differences so that they can genuinely present a united front to the congregation.

This example represents a composite of actual congregational experiences. Harmonious relationships in the parish are achievable with God's help and a commitment to work together over a period of time. The flesh will always be present in any team situation, but God's Spirit is more powerful and can bring about the kind of unity described in the New Testament epistles.

Harmonious relationships develop over a period of time as staff members get to know one another and learn to love and accept each other as God accepts them in Christ. Weaknesses and faults can be expected. Mutual love will result in bearing one another's burdens by speaking the truth in love. The staff relationships are vital because they model to the congregation how all of the Christians in that place should relate to one another.

If the team maintains a Biblical picture of harmonious relationships, God can move the staff in a positive direction. A deep and genuine unity will emerge, which will enable the team to lead the entire congregation in effective ministry.

Effective Ministry

The singular purpose for the ideal team ministry is effective ministry. Everything else serves as a means to this end. Clear expectations, a solid spiritual foundation, and harmonious relationships are intended to produce more effective Gospel ministry in the parish.

Effective ministry starts with high goals. God calls your team to equip the saints for the work of ministry. Your team disciples God's people to bring Christ to the world. Each staff member strives to give his or her best to reach these Gospel goals. You are not interested in a mere maintenance ministry or preserving the status quo. Your team wants to respond to the Gospel challenge of enabling spiritual growth in the areas of worship, education, service, and witness. All of these actions help to build the fellowship of a living, caring, outreaching body of Christ. The team spends time formulating measurable and achievable goals that will help the overall purposes of the parish to be attained. These goals will be constantly in focus. Laity and professional staff together take ownership of the goals and work together to achieve them.

The staff of a large parish school responded in the face of difficult financial times for the church by taking a look at their own stewardship response to the Gospel of Christ. Admitting some of their own wrong attitudes, they decided individually to assess their own giving patterns and rethink their promised giving. The result was a dramatic 38 percent increase in their giving as a staff. This served as an inspirational example to the congregation as a whole. High goals lead to effective ministry.

Effective ministry also involves commitment to the tasks at hand. Going through the motions to draw a salary falls far short of what is needed. Each staff member recognizes that all commitments are based on God's commitment to us in the death and resurrection of His Son. The staff member is not only committed to his or her own responsibilities but also to the staff as a whole and to the parish goals. Priorities must be formulated and human limitations recognized. God's Word and the counsel of other Christians guide in the establishment of priorities. Then commitments are made based on these priorities. As the staff shares commitments with each other, the team can be mutually supportive in honoring these responsibilities. A committed staff finds great joy in service and models that commitment to the parish as a whole. The credit and glory goes to God for whatever is accomplished, and the commitments are simply evidence of God at work in the lives of His people.

Effective ministry best makes use of commitment when the staff divides responsibilities in a helpful manner. The necessary tasks are identified. Each staff member is encouraged to search for unique gifts and abilities. Assignments are made on the basis of parish needs and staff abilities. Sometimes staff members need to perform tasks that are not comfortable to them. The staff pulls together to accomplish those tasks efficiently. Sometimes a pastor or principal tries to do everything personally rather than delegating responsibilities, but the total ministry is to be carried out by the whole parish. Staff members also seek to involve lay members in carrying out tasks. Staff members try to function in those tasks for which they are best equipped, while seeing that others are performing other tasks that they can do best.

One school staff agreed to participate fully in parish responsibilities as part of their ministry. One staff member concentrated on children's evangelism in school, Sunday school, youth group, and vacation Bible school. Two others worked with the high school youth group. Another led an evangelism training program. A fifth accepted responsibility for congregational fellowship activities, while the principal encouraged marriage and family enrichment and adult Bible study. The involvement was a real inspiration to lay leaders and provided a sense of common purpose to reach parish goals. Effective ministry was happening because staff commitment was combined with an appropriate division of responsibilities.

No team ministry is ideal. You may be struggling right now. If you are the leader as a pastor or principal, you may be frustrated because the rest of the staff seems unresponsive to your vision for the parish or parish school. You may be a staff member who feels squelched and misunderstood by a pastor or principal. You may see little hope in current staff relationships. But this book is designed to create hope within you for improved team ministry. A vital step in moving forward involves taking the time to imagine what your team could one day be like. Develop clear expectations. Build a solid spiritual foundation. Experience harmonious relationships. And engage in effective ministry.

2
Time to Practice Responsible and Accountable Leadership

STARTING OUT CORRECTLY with a team ministry is important. Picturing what the team could one day be like sets the stage for good communication and mutual respect between staff members and lay leaders. But team ministry will not work unless the staff comes to grips with the issue of leadership in the congregation. Who is in charge of what areas in what situations? Where does congregational lay leadership exert its influence? How does the pastoral office relate to congregational authority and to the other specialized teaching, youth, music or evangelism ministries by professional staff in the congregation? How is leadership shared by multiple clergy staff within the pastoral office of a congregation?

These questions are not easily answered. They have theological dimensions that most denominations address.[1] They also contain important practical considerations based on the parish context, lay leadership abilities and expectations, professional staff composition, and congregational mission. This chapter is intended to help you think through the leadership dimension of your team ministry relationship so that you can function together more effectively in a Biblical fashion to help your congregation carry out the Great Commission.

Who Leads?

Opinions differ on who should lead in a local parish and in what areas.

Three hypothetical examples will illustrate how tensions can arise when well-intentioned leadership approaches are used inappropriately in a parish.

The Pastor

Pastor Schmidt accepts a call to Grace Church. He comes with the conviction that he has the full theological truth and will properly assume the rightful authority of the office of the public ministry in that congregation. He wants to make certain that both laity and staff members in the teaching ministry give his office proper respect. He regards this strong leadership approach as essential for preserving the pure proclamation of the Word of God and the proper administration of the sacraments. He wants to show understanding and appreciation for the concerns of the parish in peripheral matters as long as they do not compromise the church's doctrinal position.

He already has his eye on the terrible practice (as he views it) of fund-raising projects in the church, especially the 50-year tradition of a sauerkraut supper sponsored by the ladies' group. He plans to wait a few months before raising strong opposition. He also opposes the elders' making calls on members, believing that only the pastor should make church calls. He wants to make sure that the school is properly run according to his church's official doctrinal position and plans to let the principal know immediately who really runs the school. Naturally he wants the principal to handle routine administrative matters and the teachers to handle their individual classrooms.

Before long, trouble is brewing at Grace Church. The congregation wants a faithful shepherd who preaches and teaches in accordance with Scripture and the church's doctrinal position. But the members find communication with the pastor to be extremely difficult. Some of their cherished customs and practices, which were intended to glorify God, are meeting with thundering disapproval. He does not seem to listen to their needs and concerns. Lay leaders feel unnecessary since the pastor appears to have everything under control. The principal feels threatened by the pastor's intrusion into the school even though the pastor appears to have few credentials as a Christian educator of children. The teachers are confused as to who is running the school and tend to develop indifferent attitudes toward the pastoral ministry. An undercurrent of opposition to the pastor begins to develop within the congregation.

The pastor more strongly mounts his righteous campaign, finding enemies of the Word of God in every quarter. He seeks more supportive lay leaders and wants to replace the principal. Lay leaders consider ways to confront the problem of an intransigent pastor. After a relatively brief ministry at Grace, Pastor Schmidt welcomes a call to another congregation that needs straightening out. Who leads at Grace? Pastor Schmidt has a clear answer that everyone in the parish hears. However, his answer does not seem to work effectively in terms of ministry at Grace.

The Principal

Mr. Braun serves as a teaching principal at Trinity Church. He has a friendly manner and wants to please the pastor, his teachers, the parents, and other lay members of the church. He believes in good relationships between staff members. A hard worker, he devotes considerable time to his teaching responsibilities. But he leaves the other teachers totally on their own. He credits them with the ability to handle their own responsibilities. Faculty meetings are infrequent and poorly planned. Responsibilities are often assigned at the last minute or forgotten altogether. Supervision is lacking. Planning is sporadic. Office work gets handled by a part-time secretary, but teachers can never be certain whether needed materials will be available. More self-directed teachers supply their classroom needs by circumventing the principal or repeatedly reminding him until the task is accomplished. Decisions are made by the group, with the most articulate faculty member swaying the rest.

No unity of purpose exists for the school. The school does not relate to the parish purpose and programs. The board of education has to assert authority beyond policy matters to keep things running smoothly. Teachers sometimes communicate their problems privately to board members.

The pastor is drawn into school problems by the board of education. Personally most people like the principal but are not certain of his directions as a leader. Who leads at Trinity School—the principal, one or two teachers, the school secretary, the board of education, the pastor? No one seems sure. Yet the principal likes his job, wants to please, and considers himself a leader.

The Lay Leaders

Zion Church welcomes its new pastor. The Schultzes and the Jungs form the welcoming committee. Longtime members of Zion and part of large family networks within the congregation, they are acknowledged leaders in the church community.

"We know you will love it here, Pastor. The members are friendly. They respect their pastors. We look to you for good, solid preaching and teaching. We need a pastor to baptize and confirm our youth, to marry and bury our members, to visit us in our homes and in the hospital when we are sick. We think you will get along well with our principal. He's been here 20 years and really knows the congregation. He can tell you what happens around here. Don't worry about anything. We have things under control. You handle the preaching, and we will run the church. If you need anything, just let us know."

Pastor Jackson soon found out what these friendly members had in mind. He had all sorts of ideas for the congregation—evangelism outreach, increased involvement in adult Bible study, a more systematic approach to stewardship growth in the congregation. They weren't interested. Congregational funds were closely controlled by the two families. Congregational participation was limited to Sunday morning. Christian education was limited to children. Boards scarcely existed. Most business was transacted informally at the Schultzes' kitchen table. Voters' meetings usually rubber-stamped what the two ruling families wanted. The principal was content to operate the school according to congregational wishes and had no desire to ripple the waters. Pastor Jackson preached his heart out about spiritual renewal in the congregation, but nothing seemed to happen. Wanting to lead in a Biblical fashion as shepherd of the flock, he experienced repeated frustration. Who leads at Zion? Pastor Jackson does in pastoral functions; the principal does in school matters; but the primary leaders are two families in the congregation.

These three examples accent important leadership issues in team ministry. Obviously pastors have leadership responsibilities according to Scripture. Congregations also have Scriptural basis for providing leadership. Other professional staff members are called to lead in their particular areas of responsibility. In practice, however, the leadership responsibilities are often abused, misused, or neglected by the parties involved. The Pastor Schmidts, Principal Brauns, lay leader Schultzes and Jungs frequently hinder the Christian mission of the church by a faulty application of leadership in the church. The remainder of this chapter will try to clarify the role of leadership in team ministry by discussing what makes a leader and how a team member leads.

What Makes a Leader?

Team relationships often suffer because no one tries to define what makes a leader. It is assumed or even stated that all team members are equal in responsibility and authority. Yet the working realities are different. This situation particularly occurs when two pastors work together in a parish as co-pastors, senior pastor/associate or assistant pastor. On the other hand, in some teams a strong effort is made to establish the senior pastor as leader with the other staff members clearly subordinate. Nevertheless, the realities of the situation often find a subordinate functioning effectively as a leader despite the formal arrangement. A leader actually functions on the basis of both authority and ability.

Authority to Lead

The authority to lead makes a leader. By the authority of his call to a congregation every pastor is a spiritual leader. The congregation entrusts to him the responsibility to preach the Word and administer the sacraments faithfully. By authority of the congregation other specialized professionals are also called or employed to exercise certain leadership functions. Lay leaders are elected or appointed by authority of the congregation through its constitution to exercise certain leadership functions. God, of course, who possesses all power, is the one who grants authority to human beings to function as leaders.

In any team ministry the formal lines of authority need to be carefully drawn and communicated. Job descriptions can be very helpful in clarifying those lines of authority. Lay leaders and professional staff work together in this process. In no way does formal authority make one team member better or more important than the other. Rather it describes roles and functions within the parish for effective ministry. The senior pastor, for example, may well have ultimate administrative responsibility. An associate or assistant pastor may be responsible for reporting to him regarding education or youth work. Yet both are called and ordained servants of the Word involved in a common ministry of Word and Sacraments. In the same way a Christian school principal has authority over the teachers in the school. They are accountable to him for their classroom performance. Yet they are equally involved in the teaching ministry of God's Word. Staff persons with authority in certain areas may lack leadership ability or the desire to lead. Yet their authority gives them the responsibility to lead as best they can.

In addition to formal authority, every team member needs to be aware of informal authority. Every congregation has its own understanding of what authority means and how it is exercised. The Schultzes and Jungs meant something different by pastoral authority than what Pastor Jackson understood. Some congregations have given great authority to their pastors even though that authority is nowhere described in writing. A staff member may gain greater authority for his position when he has served in the same parish for several years, or he may lose authority when he handles situations poorly. If a staff wants to rework traditional lines of authority to restructure the team relationship, the changes need to be processed carefully through proper channels and communicated openly at every step. The understanding of roles and lines of authority is particularly difficult when a new staff position is added with which the congregation has little experience, e.g., a second pastor, director of Christian education, deaconess, or youth director. Job descriptions are important, but much more needs to be done.

Properly constituted authority is the first ingredient for making a leader. And all staff members should preserve the established lines of authority or see that they are clearly articulated if no formal lines exist. Nevertheless, authority alone does not make a leader. Leadership ability is also important.

Ability to Lead

Leadership is both a gift of God and a skill to be learned. All staff members have occasion to lead. Many different styles can be used. The unique personality of the team member and the needs of the situation will determine the leadership style. Every staff should determine which staff members are particularly gifted as leaders. The ability to lead can then be maximized, and the team can put its best foot forward. Perhaps one team member is excellent at motivating other people. Perhaps another has the ability to plan for the future and tenaciously follow that plan. Still another may be skilled at organizing and administering the plan. Together the leadership functions are carried out. That does not need to take away from the authority and responsibility of a given team member. A gifted leader on the team can also teach leadership skills to the other team members so that each can become more effective in leadership roles. Lay leaders are often highly skilled and can help equip the professional team for more effective ministry.

The senior pastor normally will set the tone for leadership. Team members must take adequate time to get to know each other as individuals. In informal and recreational settings as well as in formal staff meetings insights about leadership values and styles can be gained. Where one is weak, the other may be strong. Team members may need to adapt to the predominant leadership style of the senior pastor if that style is accepted by the parish leadership. A perceptive senior pastor will observe and encourage team members to be themselves and to use their particular leadership styles while at the same time blending in with the parish goals and approach.

You may be a subordinate staff person with significant leadership abilities serving under a senior pastor who has authority but little leadership ability. You may feel quite uncomfortable in your team relationship. Without promising easy solutions, I would suggest that you uphold his authority and use your leadership skills to support his position from behind the scenes. As you gain his trust, he may come to appreciate your contribution to the team.

Ultimately God makes a leader. He provides the authority and the ability for a person to function in an effective and edifying manner. If the team comes to grips with the leadership issue, it can combine the members' strengths to provide dynamic leadership within the parish, working alongside and through lay leaders who have caught the vision of Gospel ministry. Pray for the two ingredients of leadership. As God grants them to you, be bold to serve. God will also show you how a team member leads.

How Does a Team Member Lead?

Granted the need for leadership in a parish and the presence of God-given authority and ability to lead, team members and lay leaders still need to wrestle with the whole process. How does a team member lead so as to cope with the excesses of a Pastor Schmidt, the neglect and ineptness of a Principal Braun, and the narrow and parochial control of the Schultz and Jung families? This section suggests three answers to the question, which provide a balanced approach to effective Gospel ministry in the parish. They apply equally whether you are a senior pastor, an assistant or associate pastor, a teaching minister, or a lay leader. How does a team member lead?

Serving

Every Christian leader must first of all be a servant. The word *minister* means one who serves. Jesus led by serving. He modeled a life of service. In the process He led the disciples into a life of ministry so that they could exercise leadership in the early church after Pentecost. His death on the cross was the ultimate act of ministry or service. In Matthew 20 He describes the rulers of the Gentiles, who lord it over their subjects. Then He exhorts the disciples: "Not so among you. Instead, whoever wants to become great among you must be your servant, and whoever wants to be first must be your slave—just as the Son of Man did not come to be served, but to serve, and to give his life as a ransom for many" (vv. 26-28).

Jesus demonstrated leadership through service when He washed the feet of His disciples in the upper room. Do not mistake Jesus' service for lack of authority or leadership. He said to the disciples on the Great Commission mount, "All authority in heaven and on earth has been given to me" (Matt. 28:18). He gave the same authority to His church, represented by the disciples. He led by serving and wants us to do the same.

Paul combines the concepts of serving and leading as part of the New Testament apostolic ministry when he writes, "Men ought to regard us as servants of Christ and as those entrusted with the secret things of God. Now it is required that those who have been given a trust must prove faithful" (1 Cor. 4:1-2). He uses the word for minister or servant as a description of the apostle and also adds that they have been entrusted with something. The word we often use for this is *steward*, which means a manager or one who rules the affairs of the household. Team members in a local parish are charged with leadership responsibilities that are to be carried out by serving.

What does this mean in practice? Pastor Schmidt rightly values the office of the public ministry and recognizes a responsibility to be a good steward of the Word and Sacraments. Apparently he fails to see himself as a servant of God and the people. They should be able to learn from his humility, personal caring for them, willingness to listen, and cooperative spirit. Then he would be leading by serving rather than lording it over them like the Gentile rulers. God's Word has also taken root in the hearts and lives of the teaching ministers and the lay leaders. They will be more faithful to the Word and better stewards of the mysteries of God if they are encouraged by his example of service. As he shares leadership with them, they are more likely to accept their God-given responsibility to lead in their assigned areas. The team will function to God's glory. Christ will be honored as the Suffering Servant who possesses all authority, and Pastor Schmidt will be revered as the spiritual leader of the congregation and a loving minister of Jesus Christ. What a contrast to the tragic situation at Grace Church and the deteriorating ministry of Pastor Schmidt!

Do you lead by serving, or are you more concerned as senior pastor that your new associate is getting too much praise from the members? Do you lead by serving, or are you bothered by your low status on the team despite your conscientious efforts? Do you lead by serving, or do you carefully guard your area of authority against other political forces in the congregation? You serve by building up the principal in the eyes of others, by giving him rightful responsibilities, and by supporting him in his work. You serve by sharing your organizational ideas and letting a team member or the team as a whole take credit for the implementation. You serve by encouraging your lay leaders to evaluate your ministry and to wrestle with important congregational directions in a planning process. You serve by getting to know your team members intimately and keeping in touch with their hopes and dreams, their problems and struggles, their jobs and families. How does a team member lead? By serving and by accepting responsibility to lead.

Accepting Responsibility to Lead

The servant role is vital for every team member, but sometimes staff members use it as an excuse for not accepting leadership responsibilities. Mr. Braun was the kind of principal who wanted to present the image of a hard-working, dedicated, caring servant who was willing to let anyone lead. He wanted all his constituencies to have the opportunity to go their own directions—pastor, education board, parents, teachers, and perhaps even the students. He prided himself in not dominating, coercing, or imposing his will on others. He was willing in a sense to wash feet. But we saw the unfortunate consequences of his inaction. The school was troubled, and almost everyone was displeased with his leadership.

In a team ministry every staff member is a leader in certain situations. Effective team ministry requires accepting the responsibility to lead. Teachers have leadership responsibilities in the classroom, with parents, with faculty committees, in certain parish activities, and in work outside the congregation in the church-at-large and the community. Church secretaries may supervise volunteers or part-time help. Directors of Christian education, lay workers, youth workers, and church musicians lead in their specialty areas and in other areas of church work. Principals and pastors have direct leadership responsibilities in a host of areas with lay and professional workers. Shirking those responsibilities will destroy the team and the Gospel ministry in the parish. A lack of leadership will produce disorganized, diffuse, and counterproductive activity on the part of other groups and forces in the congregation. Tensions, dissatisfaction, confusion, and complaining will be the result.

Taking leadership responsibility is risky. You may feel inadequate for the task. You may be uncertain about which direction to go. You may worry about the alternatives so frantically that you are prevented from doing anything. But you have the responsibility to lead in your area, and no one else can do it. It is much easier to blame the senior pastor for trying to control everything or ungrateful students for being unmotivated or lay leaders for failing to support you. But God is calling you to lead by serving and gives you the necessary authority to carry out your responsibilities.

Once you accept that responsibility to lead, you will find all kinds of help available. Your principal, the senior pastor, or a key lay leader will be glad to reflect with you and suggest helpful approaches to carry out your responsibility. People whom you lead may well have talents and gifts to complement your weaknesses and assist in the leadership. God in His Word offers you forgiveness in Christ, strength for your challenges, and direction for your task.

Principal Braun needs certain leadership skills, probably in the area of time management, long- and short-range planning, supervision, and motivation. But first he needs to accept the responsibility to lead. Recognizing the problems and his own shortcomings, grasping the potential and opportunities, he can begin to lead. The pastor, lay leaders, and even his teaching staff offer resources for gaining skills. Outside growth is also available. He can lead with a style that fits his personality. Or he may decide that he is not suited for the particular leadership responsibilities of a principal. God's direction will be clearer as he accepts the leadership responsibility inherent in the job.

Are you willing to accept the responsibility to lead? What areas call for your leadership? Are you active in carrying out your responsibilities? Do other staff members and lay leaders recognize these areas of responsibility? What problems currently plague you—your desire, abilities, skills, lack of support, problems with the group or individuals, etc.? Who might be able to help you in these problem areas? Are you using the spiritual resources available to you? Discuss these questions with your team, and share your progress with them. When each staff member leads in his/her areas of responsibility, the team functions effectively and Gospel ministry permeates the parish. How does a team member lead? By serving and accepting the responsibility to lead—and by recognizing accountability to others.

Recognizing Accountability to Others

Leadership involves the twin phrases "responsible for" and "accountable to." Every staff member is responsible for an area of leadership but at the same time accountable to another leader or group. Another way of saying the same thing is that every leader is also a follower. The president of the United States, with awesome leadership responsibilities, stands accountable to the American electorate and in some areas to Congress and the Supreme Court. The whole Watergate investigation underscored this accountability. The chief executive officer of a corporation is accountable to the corporate board of directors, which in turn is accountable to the stockholders. An Air Force colonel may hold responsibility for a large Strategic Air Command base, but he is clearly accountable to superiors at SAC headquarters, who are accountable to the Pentagon. The firing of General Douglas MacArthur by President Truman during the Korean War demonstrates military accountability in our country.

In a local parish, team ministry recognizes the same accountability. All of us are accountable to God for our entire life. He has accounted us righteous in His sight by grace on the basis of Christ's perfect life and atoning death on the cross. By faith in Christ we receive His righteousness. We are free to serve. We joyfully place ourselves under God's leadership as we live the sanctified life. As saints and sinners we recognize the need for God's leadership in our lives.

We likewise recognize the need for accountability to others in the parish. A senior pastor who leads in many areas should accept an accountability to the board of elders and the parish that he serves. A principal is accountable to the board of education. Teachers are accountable to the principal and through him to the board of education. In spiritual matters involving Word and Sacrament ministry, all team members are responsible to the pastor and through him to the board of elders. Different parishes have different external arrangements according to their constitutions. The point is that no individual is above accountability. A system of checks and balances binds called staff and laity together in a mutual arrangement.

Pastor Schmidt needed to recognize his accountability to Grace Church and its lay leadership. Schultz and Jung needed to recognize their accountability to the entire parish and to Pastor Jackson as their spiritual leader who offered guidance also for congregational directions. Team members can lead joyfully and effectively when they know where they stand and who supports them. As they properly communicate with those who exercise leadership over them, they can also serve as leaders in their areas of responsibility.

Accountability also involves informal acceptance of leadership in different situations. Although the senior pastor may have overall responsibility for the whole parish, including the school, he might choose to play the role of a follower in a faculty meeting that he attends. When the director of Christian education plans a program that involves the pastor as the teacher of a class, the pastor lets him lead. In a variety of situations each staff member sometimes leads and sometimes follows. This represents a healthy awareness of the accountability structure in a parish.

Are you willing to be accountable to your team workers, your governing boards, the members of your parish? Will you process your plans, submit your job performance, communicate your ministry to others in the parish who have responsibility for you? The process may seem difficult at first, but great benefits await your team as you affirm leadership in others and exercise leadership with others. How does a team member lead? By serving, by accepting responsibility to lead, and by recognizing accountability to others.

The time has come to practice responsible and accountable leadership in the parish. Every team needs to come to grips with the issue of leadership in the parish. Too many examples exist like those of Pastor Schmidt at Grace, Principal Braun at Trinity, and the Schultz and Jung families at Zion. Team members want to get along. They desire to work together. They respect each other's abilities. But the lines of leadership are unclear or unresolved. Who leads? No one knows, or the answer is unsatisfactory. Properly given authority needs to be established and those relationships followed. Leadership ability needs to be recognized as both a gift of God and a skill to be learned. That's what makes a leader—authority and ability. The team can grow in leadership.

How does a team member lead? He sees himself as a servant of God and of others. He dares to accept responsibility to lead in certain areas and equips himself to do so. And he recognizes that as a follower he is also accountable to others with wider leadership responsibilities. I hope you are excited about resolving the leadership issue in your midst and getting on with the exciting business of Gospel ministry!

NOTE

1. For a full discussion, see Commission on Theology and Church Relations, Lutheran Church—Missouri Synod, *The Ministry: Offices, Procedures, and Nomenclature* (St. Louis: Concordia Publishing House, 1981).

3
Starting Time Is a Time to Start

CAPTURING THE VISION of team ministry at its very best is vital to its improvement. It motivates. It facilitates growth. It is good to see that effective staff service calls for clarity in knowing what God and His church have in mind for ministry. It is good to be reminded that team ministry becomes fully viable and alive as it builds on a strong spiritual foundation and draws deeply on the harmonious relationships of its personnel. It is also good to have a fuller picture of what organized, unified, and nailed-down leadership does for the team in that vision. The realities, however, are still present.

Our team ministry strives for the ideal, but it also deals with what exists. The people, programs, and problems vary tremendously, and as a result the ministry teams are also very different from one parish to another. This chapter explores differences. It does so with the idea that each staff person joins a staff at a unique point in its development as a team. Starting time is a crucial time. It's a time to gather information, identify special factors, recognize team characteristics, and see strengths and weaknesses. It's also a time to accept fully what the present situation is in terms of structure and staff. A coordinated and synchronized starting time can enable the growth that strengthens team balance and blend.

A Church Staff Is a Church Staff

"A church staff is a church staff." Outside of its context, who could argue with Don's observation? However, when it served to downplay the importance of "teamness" for a ministry staff, it begged a barrage of rebuttal. That's what it received. Don's next evening hour was open wide enough for him to get a well-loaded, lengthy reply. He never forgot it. His pastor had taken major exception and had crisply, but kindly, explained some facts of ministry life. Thereafter, Don's parish leadership was no longer the same. He began to see the vast differences that exist between one parish staff and another. It became clear to him that the congregation with a staff that was truly a team was cooperatively, enthusiastically, joyfully, and effectively on the move with its mission.

Years later, when Don became the congregation's president, he was always sounding a clear warning every time changes were to be made on the church staff. "Ours is not just any church staff" became Don's opener. He had much to say in explanation. It was necessary for his fellow officers and members to hear and recognize that parish staff teamwork was something to be understood, to be prized, to be guarded and fed.

Congregations vary in a host of ways, and there are certainly major differences in the level of team ministry involvement from one to the next. Looking at either the quantity of parish joint staff efforts or assessing the quality of those efforts will soon illustrate the extreme poles possible. Starting time for a prospective ministry person on a staff team is an excellent time for the parish to evaluate the impact of this personnel change on its team ministry.

Drawing parallels to other kinds of team activities illustrates this. Comparing team ministry to volleyball can be almost as much fun as playing the game itself. An appropriate example is volleyball's variation of teamwork styles. There's quite a contrast between the pickup game at a picnic and the polished platoon playing down at the Y. Some church staff teams are of the everyone-for-himself, one-hit variety. Others work together. They set one another up for the spike. They talk it up when they're behind and shake it off when someone messes up a play. It is evident that much purposeful time has been put into practicing and playing because it is such a well-oiled machine.

Consider also those volleyball teams that have earnest, capable managerial leadership. It's a great game for a player-coach. Someone needs to organize the squad, or all three spikers will be in the front line at the same time. There's little quarrel from experienced church staff team players about the importance of this point. The ministry team needs leadership. Most often it will be the church's senior or administrative pastor who will provide it. Uncertainty abounds in the parish where this leadership has been neither assigned nor assumed.

As noted in chapter two, churches with major program arms will require leadership assistance for the head pastor. A parish with a school, for example, will have a principal who supervises the teaching staff. The educational and administrative expertise needed to operate a school requires its own leadership person. The same would be true of a nursery school, a day care center, or a senior citizen apartment complex.

Having a church school provides a superb area for care-filled and careful leadership teamwork. A pastor and a principal can model cooperation, communication, and competence as they go about their own and their joint administrative and supervisory responsibilities. Their colleagues will have little problem in determining which person is in charge at the appropriate times. The pastor's office calls for him to shepherd the entire congregation, and this shepherding will require him to head up the overall team as well. He ministers in this capacity, too. He doesn't meddle in the principal's everyday tasks, but he does oversee them and must be comfortable in the way things are being done. He must be able to assure himself and others that every program in the parish is operating in good order. Where co-leaders understand and respect each other and their roles and strive to be a unified ministry force, there is usually little difficulty.

The differences in the depth of commitment and activity that one can spot between parish team ministries have good reason for their existence. It is well to be reminded of the forces that shape a church staff's mentality and *modus operandi* when it comes to working together as a group.

Let's borrow four shopworn categories from the teacher's lesson-plan thinking in order to explore these forces further. If you had the responsibility of teaching a set of church workers an hour-long class on team ministry, you might mull over these four areas in order to prepare your objectives and plan. The list includes knowledge, skills, habits, and attitudes.

There Are Things to Know

Knowledge is vital to any staff's operation. Being vaguely aware of the effect of staff performance on employee morale is quite different from knowing from 10 years' experience what joy team togetherness can bring. Having an idea about what might work is not at all the same as knowing what has worked.

Test yourself on this count. Is this the first reading you are doing on the subject of church staff development, or have you read a number of books and articles about increasing the effectiveness of one's church staff?

Have you, for example, read Dietrich Bonhoeffer's *Life Together*? While the book is not specifically about staff people, it's a profound five-chapter treatise on the meaning of Christian relationships. Reading it from time to time would be powerfully helpful to anyone who is serious about Christian togetherness in staff ministry. The fourth chapter zeroes in on person to person ministry. Here's what Bonhoeffer has to say about listening:

> The first service that one owes to others in the fellowship consists in listening to them. Just as love to God begins with listening to His Word, so the beginning of love for the brethren is learning to listen to them. It is God's love for us that He not only gives us His Word but also lends us His ear. So it is His work that we do for our brother when we learn to listen

to him. Christians, especially ministers, so often think they must always contribute something when they are in the company of others, that this is the one service they have to render. They forget that listening can be a greater service than speaking.

Many people are looking for an ear that will listen. They do not find it among Christians, because these Christians are talking where they should be listening. But he who can no longer listen to his brother will soon be no longer listening to God either; he will be doing nothing but prattle in the presence of God too. This is the beginning of the death of the spiritual life, and in the end there is nothing left but spiritual chatter and clerical condescension arrayed in pious words. One who cannot listen long and patiently will presently be talking beside the point and be never really speaking to others, albeit he be not conscious of it. Anyone who thinks that his time is too valuable to spend keeping quiet will eventually have no time for God and his brother, but only for himself and for his own follies.

Brotherly pastoral care is essentially distinguished from preaching by the fact that, added to the task of speaking the Word, there is the obligation of listening. There is a kind of listening with half an ear that presumes already to know what the other person has to say. It is an impatient, inattentive listening, that despises the brother and is only waiting for a chance to speak and thus get rid of the other person. This is no fulfillment of our obligation, and it is certain that here too our attitude toward our brother only reflects our relationship to God. It is little wonder that we are no longer capable of the greatest service of listening that God has committed to us, that of hearing our brother's confession, if we refuse to give ear to our brother on lesser subjects. Secular education today is aware that often a person can be helped merely by having someone who will listen to him seriously, and upon this insight it has constructed its own soul therapy, which has attracted a great number of people, including Christians. But Christians have forgotten that the ministry of listening has been committed to them by Him who is Himself the great listener and whose work they should share. We should listen with the ears of God that we may speak the Word of God.[1]

What about the periodical literature? Have you had the opportunity to read articles such as the two that appeared in *Lutheran Education* by Walter M. Schoedel (March-April 1981) and Vernon D. Gundermann (March-April 1983)?

Schoedel, a well-known team-ministry proponent, has led highly effective multiple-staff teams for over 25 years. His article calls for a commitment from both staff and parish members to a theology (who we are), to a function (what we do), and to a plan (how we do it). It delineates roles and relationships so that team ministry can be carried on in "A More Excellent Way" (1 Cor. 12:31). That's knowledge, and we need the specific things that someone who is experienced can tell us.[2]

Gundermann, too, is relating what he has learned as a parish pastor. Titled "Teaming," his article outlines some careful thinking about staff ministry and gives straight-from-the-heart advice on how to make it successful and rewarding to individuals and to parishes. His conclusion provides the following 10 reasons for seeking out and being in team ministry:

1. It provides companionship for what can sometimes be a lonely ministry.
2. It allows for a refining and developing of special gifts.
3. It provides additional rich resources to the parish.
4. It encourages the development of one's personal faith.
5. It enables one to have more contacts with individual members of the parish, thus making possible a variety of personalities being brought to bear on the parish's work.
6. It discourages "overload" in a sharing of the ministry.
7. It supports a vision for an expanded and growing ministry.
8. It makes possible the trying, testing, and exploring of different and creative ways of doing ministry.
9. The "professionalism" of the ministry is affirmed by making possible growth time.
10. The whole church is enriched because team ministry makes available more competent resources for writing, teaching, organizing, serving.[3]

Knowing ten good reasons for being in team ministry would certainly be helpful to Gundermann were he contemplating a move to another parish. But there's more to consider than knowledge. Teamwork calls for skills, too.

There Are Skills Involved

What relational and functional skills a given parish has in its corporate bag of expertise makes a decided difference. It matters whether or not the youth minister has as much ability to plan and implement as does the minister of music. But it matters every bit as much whether or not she/he can speak and listen skillfully, conduct a meeting efficiently, or interact skillfully at someone else's meeting.

Team skills involve delegation, a key technique when it comes to getting things done through other people. Used artfully, it not only assures the effective use of staff people but can also repeatedly draw them together. Four guidelines provided in "Project: SERVE," a nation-wide skill development program for Lutheran school principals, illustrate effective delegation as follows:

1. Be sure that delegated tasks are clearly defined and that the person to whom the task is delegated is able to perform that task. Do not assign unmanageable tasks.

2. Be sure the person to whom a task is assigned knows the performance guidelines, the schedule, and the expectations of the administrator. These should be mutually agreed on.
3. Be sure that the school administrator is ready to stand by the person to whom a task is delegated with interest, help, goodwill, and commendation.
4. Be sure to give individual and public recognition for service rendered.[4]

Other accomplished skills that show up in certain teams and not in others are those related to goal setting, decision making, problem solving, and action planning. And while each team member needs these skills, it is ultimately necessary for the whole team to be trained. The volleyball squad practices serving constantly. Everyone must perfect that procedure. The effective ministry team works at its communication skills. All members of the staff are expected to have much expertise in this area, and they are simply not left to their own natural devices. These skills can be developed and fine tuned.

The knowledge about teamwork, then, can be effectively and readily put into practice as the team moves competently toward its goal. The skills of both the individual and the team point to key differences that are evident from one team to the next. Assessing "teamness" at a time of personnel change cannot help but reflect on the proficiency and dexterity of the team as it carries out its work. Observation will also bear out that the work is affected greatly by the habits that have been formed.

There Are Habits in Place

Teams do differ in the numbers and kinds of behavior patterns they've acquired through frequent repetition or repeated exposure. The habits that have become second nature to a staff carry special importance as one evaluates that staff.

Just as an individual can develop the negative patterns we call bad habits, so also can the team. The church-league softball team that follows every game with two hours at Curley's Tavern has developed an oft-accepted community practice. However, it is quite likely that the sponsoring St. Paul's Church neither planned nor expected its softball fellowship to do so. Nevertheless, joining the team and drinking beer at Curley's may go hand in hand.

A church staff's use of time may be seriously encumbered with bad habits. Any thought given to time management is likely to spawn a deluge of negative examples. There are workaholic hours at one extreme and playboy hours at the other. A church staff administrator who does not model and put into motion an appropriate balance can drive colleagues to distraction—or drive them away! The weekly meeting is monthly. The monthly newsletter is quarterly. The last annual EMV was held four years ago.

But it's the list of good habits that ought to be brought to the fore for a team to tout at new-candidate time. Are you impressed to know that the head pastor has a daily habit of 30 minutes of personal Bible study and 30 minutes of prayer? What do you think of the staff that automatically gathers for prayer the minute word is received about major sadnesses or joys? Or how do you feel about hearing that your staff-to-be has made it a habit to be prompt with meeting beginnings and ready to wrap meetings up at the appropriate closing time? What impact would the team's good habits have on your decision to join it?

Habits are signals. They point to staff patterns. They describe the team's usual state of mind. Going home for noon lunch, eating that lunch at a nice restaurant or at the church-school cafeteria, or having a brown-bag sandwich at one's office desk are all acceptable options, but any one of them might point to a habit that may not fit into an appropriate ministry mindset. That leads us to consider the fourth set of differences we could expect to find if we took the time to investigate the "teamness" of the team—its attitudes.

But the Greatest of These Are the Attitudes

Ultimately, the mental positions that team members take may tell you the most about team development and functioning. Simply wanting to be a staff of positively involved people who work together cooperatively, care about each other, and plan together in the best interest of the parish will go a long way toward having things happen that way. Having a good attitude about "teaming" will overcome a lack of knowledge about teamwork or a low level of skills for relating well or functioning well together. It will enable a team to diffuse and eradicate bad habits and build on the good practices that are in place.

The church staff certainly has an edge in the attitudes department. It has every reason to feel good about itself. It has been drawn together by God's people to do God's work. It has, in short, a divine call. The church wishes to be equipped to be the church, and it has brought a staff into being in order to equip it. What an honor! Why not function with heads held high? Why not carry on with high principles?

Why not put people ahead of programs or buildings or other things? Things can't be motivated. Things can't meet for worship or share. They can't praise or interact. A church staff team must be people-oriented. Does it have the attitude that people come first? Does it believe that ministry demands the attitude of the love-slave servanthood that Jesus so dramatically described and lived?

Why not be totally positive about what is taking place? God's staff must know and accept that the problems of people are merely opportunities for getting closer to the Lord and to one another. The warm, marvelous, cross-centered Gospel that the staff preaches and teaches is such a positive story and power. Those who live in it and proclaim it as its professional promoters surely should enjoy the positive effect it has on everything it touches.

As the team is evaluated by present and potential members, other attitudes can be spotted and noted. The following characteristics might well describe the attitude of the Gospel-centered team ministry:

1. The group seems to agree with the concept that ministry demands flexibility. They "go with the flow."
2. The team members treat people (themselves, too) as individuals, yet each still feels like an equal.
3. They appreciate people with a wide range of interests.
4. They appear to accept the fact that people come with both strengths and weaknesses.
5. This staff really prizes children!
6. Its members recognize that each staffer has to be active and productive to be happy.
7. The team obviously believes that "we're all in this together, and no one can function properly unless we all do."
8. The members already know that a fellow staffer will be able to get up if he/she fails.
9. They love to witness for the Lord!
10. "We're all here to help. Helping is our thing."

This sample description of team-ministry knowledge, skills, habits, and attitudes illustrates the depth of the mix that makes up the "teamness" of a church staff. Catching on to the characteristics involved convinces us of the importance of investing time in the evaluation of the quality of a church staff's teamwork.

One way of making that evaluation would be to use a rating scale. Constructing it would serve to point out the special elements of teamwork that are particularly valued by the parish. Using it would then identify the strengths and weaknesses of a church staff team. What follows is an example of one such evaluative tool. It was put together in order to provide the kind of scale this chapter suggests. Congregations might find the form useful as it is, or they might tailor it to fit more closely with their own conception of team ministry.

Team Ministry Quotient

Directions: Register 10 points for each of the 10 scales if the description is what your parish staff would say about itself. Reduce that number if you find the characteristic is in lesser evidence. Give it a zero if it is absent. The sum of these values is your Team Ministry Quotient (TMQ).

Characteristic	**Score**

1. The Framework of Organization　　　　　　　_____
   Our roles and responsibilities are clear. We're an orderly oper-ation. We're fairly structured. We plan. We follow plans. Our pastoral leadership is responsible, and it provides good admin-istration. We have realistic deadlines. We have established times for meetings.

2. The Channels of Communication　　　　　　_____
   We're able to be open with each other. We can be ourselves. Our communication is authentic. There's no need to be guarded or cautious. We provide plenty of printed information as we do our work. Things are understood. We provide the time to talk, and we use that time to talk. We listen with care and do well at hearing each other's feelings. We provide good feedback.

3. The Climate of Care　　　　　　　　　　　　_____
   Being rude or cross is unacceptable. We avoid giving harmful criticism. We're considerate and courteous. We make ours a pleasant place to be. We're tactful. Differences are respected and enjoyed. We're accommodating. There's no pressure to con-form. We spend time together socially, too.

4. The Mode of Ministry　　　　　　　　　　　_____
   We operate out of a servanthood style. We want to help. We expect disagreement and conflict, but we also expect to handle them well. An appropriate amount of public recognition is given to workers. We're all ministers of the Gospel, though we differ in gifts and functions. Evaluations are made, and we're up front about strengths and weaknesses. We're never manipulative.

5. The Measure of Maturity　　　　　　　　　　_____
   Our expectations are high. We put in long hours and get quality results. We grow professionally. Decisions are most often made by consensus. We're diplomatic. Our controls are from within rather than imposed. Our salaries are proportionate to our re-sponsibilities; we know what each other receives; and we're com-fortable with the differences.

6. The Unity of Purpose　　　　　　　　　　　　_____
   We have a job here that's bigger than any of us. We're committed to it. We pull together. We wish to grow spiritually. We identify,

understand, and employ clearly defined goals. We often agree on attainable, realistic, measurable objectives.

7. The Foundation of Mutual Support ____
    We respect individuality, but we're not individualistic. We not only have a genuine concern for the success of each other's programs, but we pitch in and help, too. Affirmation is important to us. We help one another get over rough spots and help each other grow.

8. The Use of Member Resources ____
    We're aware of each other's spiritual gifts. We try to make sure that competencies don't go unused. While we're always accessible, we put limits on how much we're drawn from our own responsibilities. Ours is a total parish ministry approach.

9. The Fabrics of Mutual Trust ____
    There's no room for suspicion, and we only play games for fun. We rely on each other and comfortably confide. We work at being genuine. Some risk is in order.

10. The Importance of Worship ____
    Sunday services are a matter of total staff involvement. Visibility is important. Using our spiritual gifts wisely is a must. We're apt to pray whenever we get together, and we meet for devotions on a regular schedule. Our worship is meaningful. It receives plenty of preparation.

The TMQ scale is made up of 10 elements of "teamness." While it invites introspection, it also serves as a model for the description of staff teamwork. It would be a helpful aid for the person who is charged with describing the existing team to a new candidate. When a parish is either contemplating or making a staff change, it would be to its advantage to describe itself with care. That is a crucial time for the congregation's leadership and staff administration to give special consideration to both the team that is in place and the one that is being fashioned for the future. This can begin with a statement that describes the staff as it presently exists.

The team-conscious parish seeks out its staff characteristics, sets them on the table, and sees to it that they are taken into account. It's a matter of stewardship. Time, talent, and treasure are all on the line. Bringing in a "lone ranger" is a costly venture. An individualistic staff person can hamper and harm the team, slow down its work, and reduce its effectiveness. Much energy and many hours can be consumed before the new colleague catches on and begins to blend and bond. Sometimes all the effort is for naught, and the new person soon "rides off into the sunset" toward a less demanding parish.

Wise stewardship says, "Let's be careful. Let's not just throw people together and pray. We need to know what we're all about. We have to know what we need and what we want. Let's take the time to set up a screening process that can more fully assure us of a person who will work with us for many happy and productive years."

It is the same good stewardship that ought to be practiced by any new candidate as well. How wasteful of one's own talents and abilities, of joy and satisfaction, if the new ministry post turns out to be all wrong. Count the cost of a move that disrupts a family, destroys its ties, and drops it into a congregation that doesn't become home. Consider the loss of self-esteem when a change backfires and a resignation is next year's recourse. Job deliberation time is no time simply to close one's eyes in prayer. With the Lord's help, it's a time to open them in order to see what differences exist and to pay personal attention to them. The next chapter urges the church worker to know himself or herself well. How very helpful it is to be able to recognize where one fits! How fulfilling it is when a move results in a better balance for a new staff, builds quick and lasting bonds, and brings a smooth blend of gifts and abilities.

Three Tools to Know Candidates Well

Before selecting a new staff member, the parish needs to do its homework well. Through the network of its church body offices, a congregation can usually learn most basic personnel information. There are, however, a number of additional tools that have proven useful, especially in assessing the individual's ability or penchant for teaming.

Requesting a prospective staff member to respond to a set of essay questions has been used quite extensively. The two-or-three-page form generally is accompanied by a letter that briefly explains a congregation's personnel need, asks for the candidate's permission to consider him/her for the position, and invites responses to the enclosed questions.

The following seven questions, for example, were used by an interparish school board as it sought to learn more about the people who had been suggested as candidates for its principalship:

1. Describe, please, your experience with interparish cooperation in Christian education for children, youth, and adults.
2. How would you describe the purpose of a Christian elementary school?
3. What facets of your work as a principal do you think are most important in carrying out your leadership role?
4. What do you consider your happiest moment and your most significant contribution as a Christian elementary school principal?
5. Please share what you do, or would do, to motivate a faculty to work hard and to strive for quality in its instruction.

6. Comment on the value of a staff being in team ministry and identify several things you have initiated in the past several years to strengthen teamwork on your staff.
7. How would you explain the relationship among the educational ministry of the children, parents, and teachers of a school like ours?

Parishes will generally include a number of other informational items with this mailing so that the candidates will be made more fully aware of what the congregation is like and how it perceives the position being filled. Listed below are examples of pertinent topics. Each can be addressed in a paragraph or two.

1. The congregation's mission (what we're all about)
2. The purpose of the congregation's special program arm, in case the candidate would be involved significantly because of the position—e.g., a school
3. The size of the congregation and its facilities
4. The size of the staff and a description of its "teamness"
5. The kind of community it serves
6. A description of the job's role and a listing of responsibilities
7. A description of the person being sought with a listing of the qualifications desired

Another common method for becoming more familiar with a staff prospect is the planned interview. While at times it is carried out by parish representatives who travel to the candidate's home or by a telephone call, the interview is usually done in conjunction with a visit by the candidate to the prospective parish. Such a visit has distinct advantages. It enables both candidate and parish people to see each other, and it provides for much interaction to take place. It allows for many questions and for instant clarification when an answer is unclear. More staff people can be involved. The visit can include tours of facilities and the community. A worship service can often be worked in, too. A visit by the candidate's whole family is often possible at the same time.

Interviews need to be planned. An interviewing committee should appoint a coordinator to chair the session. A checklist of the areas to be covered will assure the best use of the allotted time. This list can be refined in the committee's preinterview meeting and then serve as the agenda for its post-interview summary session.

There are some who feel that a preselection interview interferes with the "divinity" of a call. The concern often relates to the candidate's preselection involvement. Will my replies encourage the calling congregation unduly? Is the whole process too much like that of the secular world? What will my parish think? There are still times today in some churches when a person's first knowledge of the offer of a position comes with the announcement that a congregation has made the decision to call him or her. While this method can surely work, it provides no opportunity for the candidate to give input or to become oriented. The individual on whom the decision will fully rest must now begin at square one. Part of deliberation, ironically enough, is now apt to involve interview-like meetings. A preselection visit, on the other hand, eliminates much postselection explanation. The postselection visit will likely be unnecessary.

A thoughtful and caring interview for the purpose of gathering additional data is simply another form of ministry. Done with a sensitivity that aims to be God-pleasing, fair, and kind, it can maintain the objectivity and neutrality that avoids misuse and misinformation. Interviews are merely conversations and as such are time-honored tools for carrying out God's work among God's people. There need be no loss of integrity in the process.

The third tool that is used to provide the selecting body with helpful information regarding the staffer-to-be is references. This process also is enhanced by care and planning. Once again a set of questions must be written and pursued. Written references can be provided by mail, while oral references can be obtained by telephone. Both should use the same questions, however.

Those providing the references are generally people who have been selected by the candidate. Their names are a key ingredient of a personnel application form. If such a form is not used, they can be easily obtained by letter. Of special importance is some basic information regarding the length of time the reference has known the candidate and in what context. Written references, of course, must be read astutely. Church-worker colleagues and leaders can sometimes be terribly charitable to poor workers and at other times altogether too critical of those who may be doing well.

These three data-gathering methods serve as examples of what congregations are commonly doing today in order to be wise and careful stewards of the Lord's resources. All can be misused easily enough, but all can also be part of a prayerful, thoughtful, person-enhancing process that befits the people of God as they earnestly and lovingly go about the work of getting a new staff member.

And There's Orientation to Consider, Too

Understanding the present situation in the parish is also important when the new person begins his/her new tasks. There is much to learn in order to become a smoothly functioning part of both the congregational and staff machinery. The heads-up church administrator will readily recognize starting time as an excellent time for a planned approach to the orientation provided a beginning staffer.

While the rookie's needs will vary greatly from those of the incoming church-work veteran, both will be honored and assisted by the care given to them as they begin to learn the new ropes. A deliberate orientation strategy can be developed for each new staff person, and it is well to involve the present staff in developing the plan and in carrying it out.

Pastor Goodknit did it this way. He brought a beginning list of orientation possibilities for the new minister of youth to the weekly staff meeting. There it was fleshed out with additions and assignments. Emeritus Pastor Enoch was asked to cover the congregation's history. Lay Minister Stevens took Tuesday morning to handle all matters related to buildings and grounds. He included the church office procedures and getting the new staff member's own office needs in tow. Goodknit also involved lay people in the process. He had his parish president take an hour to review the official activities of the congregation during the past year and to share the new goals of the planning committee. The personnel committee chairperson had a time block during which she went over the parish policies for personnel and explained items related to wages and benefits.

Goodknit further recognized a need for orientation of the new minister's family. He and Mrs. Goodknit came up with a number of helpful ideas. They involved several lay people and several members of staff families in giving assistance and providing information.

The work of settling into a new home in a new city and possibly a new state takes a lot of energy and know-how. The ministering parish does its own "welcome-wagon" program to make the family's transition into the new community a smooth one.

In Conclusion

Starting time for the new staff person is truly a time to "think team" and to "be team." Having a clear picture of what the parish staff is like will greatly reduce the difficulties involved in decisions and moves. Team ministry is very different from one congregation to the next. It needs to be understood and communicated to would-be and will-be staffers on the personnel horizon. The sound and sincere investment of time at the beginning of a ministry will reap rich dividends, including a happier, more fulfilled ministry and a happier, better-served congregation.

NOTES

1. Dietrich Bonhoeffer, *Life Together* (New York: Harper and Row, Publishers, 1954), pp. 97—99.
2. Walter M. Schoedel, "Pastor-Principal-Teacher Relationships: A More Excellent Way," *Lutheran Education* 116 (March-April 1981): 199—203.
3. Vernon D. Gundermann, " 'Teaming,' " *Lutheran Education* 118 (March-April 1983): 217.
4. Aid Association for Lutherans, *Project SERVE: Lutheran Schools,* Operations Manual (Appleton, Wis., 1982).

4
Taking Time
to Know Myself Well

WE HAVE SEEN how church ministry teams vary. When a new staffer comes on board, it is helpful to note these differences and take them into account. There is a "teamness," and this propensity to work together can be enhanced as it is promoted through organized, democratic leadership. It can grow as the team becomes more aware of what it takes to be a team and proceeds to garner skills that are certain to help. It will become a more responsive and responsible team as it recognizes the importance of habits and attitudes.

As the team works hard to understand and improve itself, it will be constantly faced with a parallel challenge. The individuals on the team must each personally struggle to know what they are all about when it comes to being team persons. As a staff member becomes more aware of what makes the team work, this awareness becomes a special strength to use for the good of the team. It's a plus that can be developed to a greater degree and can help carry the team in certain ways.

A baseball pitcher who leads his team to victory after victory was once a youngster who simply wanted to play ball. Someone had to spot and motivate him. Coaches were necessary in order to teach skills and to fend off bad habits. Experience had to come in order to turn potential into reality.

Above all, however, the "kid" had to know that he could pitch. He had to believe that some day he'd be able to grind out a whole batch of successful innings. Once he knew that his speed could leave someone swinging, and once he could target where the ball was to go, his confidence began to build. He knew himself. He could pitch. He no longer had to worry that much about his lack of hitting ability. He'd stop trying out for shortstop.

The pastor who can really preach is a lot like that pitcher. His pulpit is his mound. He's very much the center of Sunday attention. The team gives him the go-ahead. He'll deliver more sermons than the team's other pastor, and the rest of the team will even help him get better. They'll also attend to those tasks that the pastor is unable to do because of his preaching load. But remember, this excellent sermonizer and speaker also had to get over some initial confidence humps. He had to get to know himself and to be free to try and free to fail. He had to be encouraged and coached.

The job is clear. A church staffer needs to take time to know himself/herself. This chapter opens up that "can of worms" because this is so important for staff teamwork. Though it's a cursory treatment of the subject, it serves as a reminder and as a touchstone. The task of knowing oneself well is monstrously huge. It is one of the greatest challenges any person can face; to know oneself thoroughly is the quest. One can be amazingly unaware of who she/he is in certain contexts. A person doesn't fully realize or appreciate, for example, how easily another person is affected. A brief word or look can set someone off. We may be quite unable to explain why we cause certain reactions in our workmates. We also may be unable to tell a colleague why she/he affects us or how it takes place.

There's much to learn about our impact on those with whom we work. It's an education that can seemingly remain hidden for an entire career, or it can begin to emerge early. But it surely will be ignored unless some special "time-outs" are taken to address and consider it. Let's realize that just like any other learning chore, taking a course about oneself can be concentrated into a small period of time if facilitated by the right materials or teachers and made more meaningful through appropriate conditions.

Brett was a ministry-minded young man who became a director of Christian education after a brief career as a teacher. After a poor first year in his new position, and assisted by the wise counsel of his head pastor, he decided to undergo a series of thorough interviews and tests by a group of vocational consultants. It was an eye-opener for him. In a matter of hours he learned some very surprising things about himself. Most revealing was his lack of interest and skill in the area of administration. It was small wonder he had so much trouble with some of his plans and programs. He began to see things about his ministry as a director of Christian education that were different from his days as a teacher.

The classroom provided Brett with a schedule. He had to be ready when school opened and classes began, and he was. As a director of Christian education, however, no one was telling him that he had to be in at 8:00 and home by 5:00—and he wasn't. He did not enjoy office hours. He couldn't get himself to put together any directions for the church secretary. He hadn't learned to tell anyone in the office that he was making a house call and wouldn't be in. It never occurred to him to have a plan for when he'd be back.

Brett discovered a lot about himself quickly. It almost wrecked his ministry, but his helpful staffmates came through in very supportive ways. Adjustments were made. The church office secretary became a firm but kind combination of mother, mentor, and staff sergeant. His administrative pastor headed up a review and revamping of his job description. Brett eventually returned to the classroom, but his remaining years as a director of Christian education were quite happy and successful ones.

Oddly enough, for many church workers who are having a frustrating and unfulfilling ministry, a crisis of considerable note must arise before that kind of learning about oneself takes place. At times, the I'm-not-sure-why-but-I'm-resigning-anyway action comes first.

For other staff members, however, it may take many years of counseling in order for them to begin to understand what has caused them to be dissatisfied, disturbed, or distressed with their work. It takes much effort—for both the client and the counselor—but if there's a willingness to learn, time will provide answers. Norman's self-evaluation eventually led him to write the following:

> I'm not very communicative or all that friendly. I seem to want to compete rather than cooperate. I'm not very patient, and I do like to find fault in others. I seem to have the results I want in people well in mind far in advance. I won't verbalize them right away, but I'll get them on the table at just the time when I can most likely tap the readiness of others. I'm beginning to see that I'm not really a democratic person at all. I've always spoken against authoritarian approaches, but for some reason that's what I seem to prefer.

While Norman had many reasons for his unhappiness on the church staff, he had repeatedly attributed them to his co-workers. One after another they received his critical barrages. It was always someone else's fault. Full and healthy change did not come for him until he could say, "I think I now know who I am."

An Opening Exercise

Although knowing oneself is complicated and at times requires professional assistance, church workers must think of it as yet another way in which a person needs to be growing steadily and regularly. Deliberate attention to the task surely helps. Drawing three circles, for example, can help explain some of the difficulty involved and serve as a good introductory exercise.

Label the first circle "My Me." This is your view of who you are. Under this circle you can begin to list words to describe yourself—understanding, kind, warm and affectionate, patient, a bit too trusting, demanding at times, poor about deadlines, somewhat afraid to confront, enjoys attention.

Call the second circle "Others' Me" and recognize that your fellow workers may well describe you differently. What if their list includes words such as "inconsiderate, calculating, disinterested, uncaring, a little flaky"? Major descriptive departures from your list may be unlikely from staff members who know you well, but they are certainly to be expected from the person who has just begun working with you.

Then tag the third circle "The Real Me" and realize that still another list now needs to be written. No human being, of course, could actually come up with it. Some would love you too much to even begin writing the telltale words. Others may not care enough to even think about it. The list is nevertheless a reality. There is a real you, one you really ought to know and enjoy and more fully actualize.

The healthy ideal in all this is to imagine that the three circles could be drawn right on top of each other. Some psychologists have borrowed a descriptive term from the mathematicians and called this picture-perfect idea *congruence. Being real* captures the concept, too.

Getting Close to Myself

Being very close to oneself is yet another way to describe this sought-after congruence. It is more easily understood when it is compared with a relationship between two people. One is bound to have problems with a friendship in which two people are separated by great distances. Travel is difficult. Long distance calls are expensive. Letters are hard to write. They simply don't spend the necessary time on this relationship. If they were closer in terms of physical distance, it would help them keep stronger bonds. If they were closer in terms of relational strength, it would make the bonds stronger in spite of the miles. It's not hard to think about closeness in these two ways—actual distance and strength of relationship—and see how both affect interpersonal relationships.

The differences that closeness makes are clearly demonstrated in families. Think about the strong relationships developed by the parents who hug their children, the husband and wife who hold hands, the family that sits together in church, the two brothers who play catch for endless hours, the sisters who work at the same restaurant. An argument or rift between family members is almost always going to create distance between them. A wife and husband locked in a not-talking spat will deliberately avoid touching. The distance between them in bed is a canyon. That is not so, however, when forgiveness reunites them. Closeness is a strong sign of healing.

If closeness can be such a definite aid to ties between two people, why should it be any less powerful for a person who gets closer to himself? Getting to know oneself has been seen universally as a strong contributor to wholeness, to being contented with one's lot and happy with one's life. Why shouldn't closeness to oneself also be helpful to the team on which one serves?

The "Who am I?" question might well be answered, then, in another way. As a member of a ministry team I have a responsibility to become steadily more aware of who I truly am. I will do so in the hope that this closeness, this unifying of who I think I am with who I really am, will serve me in good stead in all my relationships.

Self-Closeness Aids the Team

There are specific pluses that I can list as I think about self-closeness and team ministry. Knowing myself well should result in better decisions. I should be able to make little adjustments and changes that can improve my ability to relate to others or to do team tasks. I ought to be able more wisely to offer myself for ministry jobs that suit me. I'll be able to blend into the ministry team more effectively. Because I will know my strengths and weaknesses better, I will become more effective in my work as I use my strengths and shore up my weaknesses. I'm more apt to accept my differences and to appreciate the differences in others. In short, my becoming closer to myself will allow me to minister to myself in better ways.

My ministry to me is not to be thought of as self-centeredness. It's quite the opposite. Through my closeness to myself, I'm apt to grow in appreciation of what God has created in making me a living being. As I grow to like and accept myself, a healthier, more mature person is bound to emerge, one who will better serve the Lord and the people around him.

Knowing Myself Spiritually

God most assuredly directs me in my search for congruence. His Scriptural words cause me to come back repeatedly to my "I am-ness." He firmly but gently leads me to recognize truths that impact my life, truths that I really have to know.

I'm a sinner. Evil and wrong are second nature to me. I can so easily harm and hurt, prevaricate and pilfer. Selfishness is just under the surface. It's right next to anger, greed, prejudice, and hatred. My mind's capacity to misuse sex, to covet material goods, and to doubt God's love is just a click away.

And you're one, too. Your list can't compete with mine—that is, not when I'm making one out for me. But you know your list, and what you know of that list makes it the worst you know. You know your blindness and blight. You're keenly aware of what you lack. There's love that is puny, respect like a wrinkled raisin, care that blossoms in a moment but has petals that fall to the ground two days later.

And what about the others, the rest of the team? They are sinful beings, too. They battle laziness just like we do. They give in to cheating and gossip. Despair and fear can grab them in a moment. Cynicism and indifference lie in wait. Self-preoccupation is so often their theme of the day, and how very weak is their prayer, praise, and giving of thanks.

But there's more to the story. We know it well, too. It's a marvelous message, one that is all the more a thing of beauty when it is set next to our sin. It's God's story. Out of an interest that we can neither fathom nor fully describe He created the world and its inhabitants. He has made us in His image, created us to be perfect representations of Himself. And He still wants that for us. Our being born in the death-like grip of sin has not deterred our Father, the Creator. From the time of Adam and Eve He has sought to restore us. Our lives are wrapped in His reach, His grace. He wills for us to have His power. In an unbelievably persistent manner He pursues us, dropping Himself in our paths so that we can't help but see Him, know Him, respect Him, and love Him.

Our Bibles show us that He's been working in the lives of people for all time. He rescues and reclaims. His plan of love not only creates—it renews. It caused Him to send His Son into the real world as a real person while He was still also that very real Son. Jesus was His name. He came into the world of people to be their Redeemer. His earthly life would lead Him to a real death and resurrection that would provide us with redemption through His blood, even the forgiveness of sins. He brought us new birth and new life. Our Father not only pursued us to the point of giving us a new and clean start, but He has also stayed after us and with us with His Holy Spirit. It is the Spirit who gets us to look to Jesus as Lord and who seals our faith relationship to God in Jesus' reclaiming work. We have His Word on it. He has given us His Word to assure us and bond us and keep us. We read and hear and share His marvelous Gospel, and the Holy Spirit goes to work. He convinces us. We are rebuilt in His power. He takes up residence in our hearts and defends our faith and nurtures it for a new life that can daily repent and receive, a new life of service to our Triune God and to the people He has dropped around us.

Live the New Life as an Imitator of God

This new life of the person who is in Christ is described nicely in Paul's letter to the Ephesians, and his description calls for us to see ourselves as imitators of God. In the third chapter he explains that God made him a minister "to preach to the Gentiles the unsearchable riches of Christ" (v. 8) and to explain to everyone that all people have been saved "according to his eternal purpose which he accomplished in Christ Jesus our Lord" (v. 11). Then Paul prays that the Ephesians will come to know God's power in their lives, "so that Christ may dwell in your hearts through faith" (v. 17). Then he asks that they, "being rooted and established in love," might be able to feel and understand God's love fully and experience this love so that they may be "filled to the measure of all the fullness of God" (v. 19). Then Paul notes that God has given gifts to certain people to be His ministers in order "to prepare God's people for works of service, so that the body of Christ may be built up" (4:12) and to have them "in all things grow up into him who is the Head" (v. 15). He then goes on to describe the new life in Christ in the rest of chapter four. This leads to his words of direction: "Be imitators of God, therefore, as dearly loved children" (5:1).

Imitating Jesus

Just as Jesus lived on this earth in the image of His heavenly Father, imitating Him in every respect, so also I live the new life in order to imitate my heavenly Father. The Holy Spirit empowers me to do so. I truly need to be like God. I seek after His purity and truth, His generous giving and gentleness, His forgiving mercy and love. As one of His beloved children I will imitate my God, and no better model can I find than Jesus Christ, His true Son.

Among the many ways in which I can view the Jesus I wish to imitate is to think of Him as the "Christ of the creative response." Over and over again the Scriptures show us a Jesus who makes deliberate and creative decisions. A few loaves and fish fed thousands, while a few words expelled a devil or formed an appropriate parable or silenced His critics. Jesus made room for children, made a whip to drive the money changers from the temple, and made 10 lepers well. He saw problems, and He responded to them with clever, creative, and capable actions. He surely calls on all who imitate Him to address their tasks with plans and actions that are imaginative, intelligent, and ingenious.

Use Your Imagination

One imaginative way in which the church staff person can learn more about himself/herself is to dream about the world of nonchurch vocations. What would I be if I were not a pastor? Would I make a fine accountant, or would I be better at selling cars? Could I be a good plumber or carpenter, or would I have to be a foreman and manager?

What would I, ponders a church school teacher, have to offer the secular world of work? Could I write news articles or commercials for a living? Might I do a good job of training insurance salesmen? Would I be best at working with little children, or could I deal with youth and adults? How would the police department use me? What is there that I do so easily and well that would cause many an employer to hire me on the spot?

The imagination can also project a church staffer into other ministries than the present one. "If I were a pastor," says a teacher, "I'd make great hospital and house calls. My sermons probably wouldn't be the greatest, but I'd sure do well as a counselor and friend." Imagination can draw us out of workaday ruts by providing worthwhile suggestions for new ministry tasks that can be done within the context of our present job.

What we are suggesting is that a church staffer can learn a great deal about who she/he is if some time is set aside to think and dream, to consider honestly and creatively what nonchurch vocation would be possible. One's imagination will serve remarkably well to skirt the tasks that need to be avoided and to court the work that can be done with ease. It can help us see who we really are.

Use Your Intellect

Intelligence can also be enlisted in the pursuit of self-understanding. There are well-developed and sensible evaluation procedures that knowledgeable analysts have presented to us for our own intelligent appraisal.

One procedure in particular is important because of the special impact it can have on church workers. It is generally referred to as the discovery of spiritual gifts. While the basic knowledge that God gives gifts to those who are in the body of Christ is as old as the three key Bible chapters that list such gifts (Romans 12; 1 Corinthians 12; and Ephesians 4), it has only been during the last decade that much has been written to describe the possibilities involved in discovering and developing spiritual gifts.

C. Peter Wagner wrote an important book on discovering spiritual gifts, *Your Spiritual Gifts Can Help Your Church Grow*. It provides a thorough and easily understood description of what these gifts are, how a Christian can identify the one or more that God has given, and how such gifts can be used more effectively in the church.

What are your spiritual gifts? Do you, for example, have the gift of leadership? Can you claim the gift of administration? Or do you have the gift of helps or hospitality? Is yours the gift of teaching or evangelist? The latter is described by Wagner as follows:

> The gift of evangelist is the special ability that God gives to certain members of the Body of Christ to share the gospel with unbelievers in such a way that men and women become Jesus' disciples and responsible members of the Body of Christ.[1]

He also recommends what a person should do in order to determine whether she/he has such a gift. "The process of discovering this gift is the same as that for any other. Experiment, examine your feelings, evaluate your effectiveness, and expect confirmation from the Body."[2]

Based on such guidelines, other churchmen have devised useful tools that can assist a person in knowing what spiritual gifts she/he has been given. David W. Hoover and Roger W. Leenerts did this in a lengthy Bible study they published in 1979. It concludes with a five-page questionnaire that serves as an inventory of 21 spiritual gifts and feeds into a personal profile graph. It helps point out the special strengths provided a believer by the Holy Spirit, gifts that can surely make a difference to a team ministry situation.[3]

A church staff's effectiveness can be greatly enhanced as it begins to know each minister's gift mix and to understand its own picture of spiritual giftedness. Certain members will identify gifts that have been ignored. Others will rejoice in knowing more fully what they were somewhat sure of before. Some will find that they have no gift to help them in areas of major responsibility. What a great opportunity for a church staff to work as a team in order to blend its strengths and overcome its weaknesses!

An article by Kent Hunter in *Leadership* describes one church staff that diligently worked at discovering their gifts and then exercised them in their duties. For this group of church workers the process served as an excellent way to alleviate staff tensions and to lead to healthy, functioning, effective team ministry. Hunter provides 10 practical steps for managing a church staff on the basis of spiritual gifts.[4]

Use the Ingenious Instruments, Too

One who is sincere in better understanding himself can employ other instruments, too. Some are quite ingenious in the way they gather, interpret, and implement data. Those that have been published tend to be research based. At times they are devised for local and limited use, such as for a citywide conference program, while there are also instruments that appear on the pages of national magazines or journals. They can be useful for the signals toward self-understanding that they give, for the patterns that they seem to suggest.

An especially appropriate tool for someone involved in team ministry may be one that provides information on a person's behavioral style. Whether at work, at home, or at a favorite place of recreation, one is likely to think, feel, and act in a fairly consistent manner in each of these settings. It can be helpful to have this pattern of behavior identified and analyzed. Seeing oneself more clearly in this way can provide the necessary motivation for change. Behavioral style can be modified if a person begins to see good reasons for doing so. The change involved could greatly enhance the effectiveness of the workplace team.

Such a tool was developed by Dr. John G. Geier and was first published by Performax Systems International in 1977. It is entitled *The Personal Profile System* and describes itself as "A Plan to Understand Yourself and Others."[5] The instrument is not a test. Rather, it is a 12-page tool that measures perception of self along important dimensions of behavior and identifies behavioral patterns. Specific tendencies toward strengths are described, as are tendencies toward weakness if the strengths are overextended. The challenge for the individual is to increase an understanding of self and others and to apply this knowledge either to the work environment or to a social or personal environment. Various behavioral strengths can be seen as personal dimensions on which to build. On the other hand, weaknesses may be causing conflicts with others. Knowing these limitations better can assist in efforts to overcome them. Becoming more adept at blending the differences in staff styles of behavior will lead to increased harmony and productivity.

Another example of a helpful appraisal device is the *Meyers Briggs Type Indicator*,[6] which is used often today for in-service staff development to help individuals improve intergroup communication. It enables a participant to learn about typology of personality, to identify his/her own personality type, and to begin applying the type theory in order to upgrade staff interaction and communication.

Instruments such as the profile and the type indicator would be most effective when administered by a trained leader in a workshop setting. Others are designed as self-applied tools. In general, they work because thoughtful input has been pulled together, expanded to facilitate understanding, and personalized to enable application. There are, of course, many other ways in which a person can obtain fruitful feedback for self-understanding.

Be Creative About Getting Other Feedback

The search for a closer relationship with oneself can often miss out on feedback from the most obvious of sources. How often will a teacher ask the class to evaluate his/her instruction or discipline? Yet, it is not hard to imagine that the feedback would be valuable. Does the parish pastor set aside some time to sit with the office secretary just to hear a description of his everyday work style? A thoughtful, alert secretary will have little difficulty in describing what she has come to know as the pastor's style of office behavior. The possible ways for obtaining information about oneself are numerous if we become more serious and less fearful about getting this feedback and more attuned to using creative methods for doing so. The following are a few suggestions a person might find useful:

1. Write a letter of reference for yourself as if a prospective employer had

requested it. Pretend that you are a close colleague. Let your spouse or special friend read it and react to it in order to improve the observations made.

2. When vacationing at your parents' home, ask them to show photographs, slides, or movies of your childhood and youth. Encourage them to relate things about your past. You could also find out a lot about what you were like by interviewing a parent about your past with the use of a tape recorder. Making a tape brings out the best in such interviews, while the tape becomes a precious remembrance of an enjoyable conversation and a valuable record of family history.

3. Request the members of a board with whom you have worked for a goodly period of time to read your job description and to evaluate your effectiveness. Devise a four- or five-point scale they can use to facilitate the task.

4. Invite a perceptive, well-adjusted friend, perhaps a church staffer from a neighboring parish, to shadow you at work for a day or two. Conclude the observation period by having him/her share with you a description of your work style.

5. Have your colleagues at work each describe you through the use of continuums such as those found in certain behavior description questionnaires. (See Appendix C for a sample instrument.)

6. Develop the habit of concluding certain family or staff projects with a sharing-caring circle. Have one person in the circle say what she liked most about each of the others involved. Have each of the rest go around the circle in the same way.

7. Buy the Ungame and play it with family and friends. Its cards frequently call for players to share observations about fellow participants.

8. Put thoughtful time into reading and using *The Caring Question*,[7] a book by Don and Nancy Tubesing that will help you strike a healthy balance between caring for yourself and caring for others. It provides a host of thought-provoking questions, useful checklists, and practical suggestions that will guide you to view good health from the spiritual, mental, and relational perspectives as well as the physical.

9. Read Jess Lair's *I Ain't Much, Baby—But I'm All I Got.*[8] It's enjoyable and easy to read, a book that will help you share in the success of finding yourself.

10. Attend a workshop or take a course that deals with improving communication or strengthening relationships. One church minister friend found that he made tremendous strides in self-understanding by going through a leadership training course. While they were quite unrelated to church work, the lessons fostered personal understanding and growth

that clearly strengthened his confidence. He became a more effective minister as a result.

Through our own deliberate efforts we can grow closer to ourselves. We can become our own best friends. We can treat ourselves kindly and steadily increase the respect and love for the person we have been created to be. Self-awareness will help us handle difficult matters. We'll also be more realistic about what tasks we can take on and complete. Greater satisfaction will follow.

Those on the ministry staff who have made such gains will covet them for fellow workers as well. As they model fuller measures of contentment, confidence, and control, they will provide healthy examples for colleagues to follow. Their kindly cautions, sober suggestions, and thoughtful praise will help eliminate the useless put-downs, needless worries, and senseless pressures that can so easily accompany a minister's life. Sound and solid mental health and maturity for the co-worker becomes the added ministry goal each staff member has for the next.

Taking time to know myself well is done within the context of knowing that I am the unfinished clay and my heavenly Father is the potter. He continues to carefully and surely form me in every respect, while I confidently continue to trust in His love and strength to do so. The time I take to know myself well will always help me to see His creative and powerful hand at work and to recognize fully how Christ's constant forgiveness provides me with His power.

I'm a person God prizes, prepares, and empowers. He has special plans for me, and they include serving happily, cooperatively, and effectively in His body, the church.

NOTES

1. C. Peter Wagner, *Your Spiritual Gifts Can Help Your Church Grow* (Glendale, Calif.: Regal Books Division, G/L Publications, 1979), p. 173.
2. Ibid.
3. David W. Hoover and Roger W. Leenerts, *Enlightened with His Gifts* (St. Louis: Lutheran Growth, 1979).
4. Kent R. Hunter, "A Model for Multiple Staff Management," *Leadership* 2, no. 3 (Summer 1981): 99—107.
5. *The Personal Profile System* (Performax Systems International, Inc., 1978).
6. *Myers Briggs Type Indicator* (Palo Alto, Calif.: Consulting Psychologist Press, Inc., 1976).
7. Donald A. Tubesing and Nancy Loving Tubesing, *The Caring Question* (Minneapolis: Augsburg Publishing House, 1983).
8. Jess Lair, *I Ain't Much, Baby—But I'm All I've Got* (New York: Fawcett Crest Books, 1972).

5
Putting Time into Improving Relationships

RELATIONSHIPS MAKE LIFE meaningful. A bond is made. Giving occurs. Giving up is part of it, too. As time passes, the desire to give deepens. Threads braid together to become a stout cord. A welding of wills takes place. While negative unions gnarl and cripple, a positive partnership like a happy marriage adds purpose to life. For Christians the covenantal faith in Jesus Christ as Savior and Lord provides the optimal example of relationship and worth.

The church facilitates and nurtures that bond of faith in God, who gave and gives as no other can or will. The church enables and nurtures relationships from one member to another as well. The people of God pull together, serve together, and grow together as the bride of that same Jesus Christ. The organized church is a custodian of relationships, the most vital imaginable, and it calls pastors, teachers, and others to help it accomplish this service in the best possible way.

Whatever a ministry team's size or experience, background or qualification, it exists to lead and feed and weed artfully, lovingly, and wisely, so that the people of God relate fully and well to their heavenly Father and to each other as His redeemed and Spirit-led pack. The church staff equips for unity, prays for it, and pleads for it. It recognizes itself as model, too, and teaches of Christian bonding with its example.

It follows then that the collection of people called and designated to be a congregation's shepherding staff will be equipped, anxious, and willing always to improve the relationships that help it minister as a Christ-centered team.

This chapter offers a thoughtful, thorough, yet practical series of hints and suggestions. It wishes to build the reader's awareness so that enough is grasped about a given idea to associate it with staff relational needs and to suggest possibilities for bettering the bonds of the team. Within the lines are both the whys and what we purport to be wise. Between the lines we hope there breathes the winsome invitation and warmth of a cordial koinonial climate.

Pointing Out Some Stars

A group of teachers from a number of parish elementary schools was being quizzed during an after-school joint session dealing with staff relationships. The comments that follow were written on three-by-five-inch cards in response to the question, "Which of your colleagues do you feel closest to and why?"

I really feel good about Tom. When he says something, I know that I can believe it.

Kris knows me. She can even point out my mistakes and it doesn't bother me. I appreciate her a great deal.

You know you've been listened to when you talk to Don. His whole being seems to strain at hearing what you say and if he isn't hearing it, he's bound to pump you further.

I like Pastor Renner a lot. He's so real all the time. For example, I can fully enjoy any of his words of commendation. I know he's giving out genuine praise. He's never just trying to flatter you in order to butter you up.

Ruth's great. She seems to really understand the importance of feelings. No matter if I'm frustrated or depressed or if I'm super happy or just feeling satisfied, she listens to my emotions as well as my words.

It doesn't matter how busy he is, I always feel that Howard has time for me, and I know how busy a principal can be. It's neat to be in a school that topbills its teachers.

You can count on Sarah to make you smile almost any time she's around. She's got a great sense of humor and she's willing to use it even when she's tired or running late.

Even though these were off-the-cuff observations, the teachers' offerings pointed to the skills, conduct, and attitudes that are important in the matter of relationship building. You can trust Tom and Kris—he's honest; she cares. Don's a good listener, and the pastor is authentic. Ruth has learned to value feelings, while Howard values people, and Sarah puts a premium on perking up others with some humor.

What was also present in this list of prized personal qualities was the unmistakable element of time. Going out of one's way to listen well or to speak with care takes extra thought, extra effort, and extra energy. When you're in a hurry or flippant or tired, you're more apt to interact less satisfactorily. Time is a vital ingredient in the process of relationship building.

That truth is plenty obvious to the college senior who carefully composes his letter to the woman he plans to marry next summer; it takes a long time to say what he wants to say. It's clear to the busy woman who drops by to visit her own aging and lonely mother; it takes time to have a good conversation. It's plain to the second baseman that he has to spend time with the shortstop. Relationships dry up without letters and calls and conversations and being together.

Time is the hose and sprinkler that convey the life-giving water of communication to the intended. The caring gardener brings the hose out of the garage, hooks it up, and turns on the faucet. Were she uncaring, the relationship would instead be left to the whims of the passing weather. The rains might water well, but they might also gush down and erode or drown, or there could be dry spells and drought. A church staff is as vulnerable a garden as any family or other meaningful group.

Two Operational Principles

Two important operational principles are at work. One might be called "Contrive and Pursue," while the other we have tabbed "Perceive and Capitalize." Both may seem terribly obvious. We deal with them routinely and often in our various relationships. Though they are obvious, they are not to be ignored. How we understand and use these two controlling facts of relational life can make vast differences. Both are important.

Let's first consider the *contrive-and-pursue principle*. It stands ready to go into effect the moment a need begins to emerge. As that need becomes clearer, it begins to ask that something be done about it. Sometimes the need is allowed to grow until it demands that something be done; then the need has become a problem. However, when people recognize that the problem can be picked up in stride and understood and viewed as an opportunity, a solution is soon carefully fashioned. An invention has been made. A new contrivance will address the problem and work it out all right.

Now we must give our solution the legs to help it get somewhere. It needs an administrative design. Tasks are identified and assigned; a time line is hatched; and someone is put in charge. We devise and design. We contrive and pursue special experiences that will satisfy a need or solve a problem that has arisen within the staff.

The *perceive-and-capitalize principle* will also be in effect. It is based on the premise that as a group of people go about their work, they will be affected by a constant flow of events. Many of these will have the earmarks of bonding experiences, relationship-building possibilities. Will staff members take the time to incorporate what has popped up for them or will they ignore it?

Consider this list: A workshop is offered by district leadership. An article appears in a journal. A colleague becomes seriously ill. An anniversary of the parish is coming up. An invitation from a college asks that its student evangelism team spend two work weeks in the congregation. A staff member has agreed to speak at another parish when he was already booked solidly in his own. How these occurrences are viewed and whether or not someone will capitalize on them in order to help build staff relationships will make the difference.

Something happens. An experience has become available. When the event is seen as a positive way to enhance the kinship between members of a team, the whole staff or one of its members will take advantage of it in some way or to some extent.

Seeing the possibility comes first. One staff may be more ready, aware, and open to a growth opportunity than another. Second, it will take time. Will it fit in? Does anyone care whether it fits in? Do we have the administrative leadership to make the most of it at this time? Are we already too overextended to be able to do it? Even the time the staff uses to consider it can be seen as a growth opportunity. Often there is precious little time to decide. The staff that cares more deeply about its relational bonding is bound to see more possibilities, to have more bonding experiences, and to grow closer to each other. It will allocate more of its available time to the care and feeding of itself as a ministry unit.

Devising an actual bonding experience and capitalizing on activities to provide bonding experiences are to be viewed as ministerial activities. They are addressed thoughtfully, lovingly, prayerfully. They are carried out artfully and skillfully. But they are not done in order to gain advantage over the sister or brother. They are not mechanical or manipulative processes. They are contrived and put into action as ways of ministering to the relationships that tie staff members together in an effective unit.

When parish administrators realize the value of deliberately setting up time for staff relational development, visualize a workable and sensible plan, and then organize that precious time to nurture the relationships among members of a church staff, they can count on a collage of bountiful crops. This is enhanced by yet another operational rule. While a deliberately planned effort may have been designed to improve just one aspect of staff relational development, a much wider set of relational elements will be affected. People defy compartmentalizing. They are too complex. Pursuing one aspect of relationship building is bound to affect other elements and have numerous spin-offs. It snowballs. The gravy will be there. Having a pervasively positive attitude about the specific activity involved will result in by-products that will also tend to be more positive. Meanwhile, a specific goal can be met as it is specifically addressed.

There are many possibilities that can be pursued. Four illustrations are given in this chapter. To demonstrate more fully how a staff can capitalize on occurrences and to show the unplanned pluses that happen at the same time, four other examples are described that will motivate certain church staff people to engineer relational additions or revisions to the annual or weekly calendar or to the daily schedule. They will motivate other staff people to accept such attempts, to help make them work, or to suggest other improvements.

You Can Pursue Growth of Interdependence

One brief but well-planned annual August meeting between the custodial staff and the teaching staff will do wonders. The agenda might allow each to state its expectations of the other. Some conflict is to be expected. Give and take will ensue, and a happy consensus is likely. A healthy interdependence will be fostered and years of griping averted. Someone saw the possibility for a package of time and planned for it to happen.

You Can Pursue an Accrual of Support

Senior Pastor Proe and Associate Pastor Conn eat lunch together every Thursday in the school cafeteria. They decided to do this last September as a weekly way to discuss their differing views about the parish's elementary school. Conn may continue to doubt the school's full value as an arm of the congregation, but Proe has given him a lot to consider. Conn has heard out his administrator. He understands. He'll support the staff leader's strong interest in the school with the rationale that has been carefully explained to him over the course of the school year. Their relationship keeps improving, and they are better able to support one another as they carry out their work.

You Can Pursue Perception-Checking Skills

Dr. Morton values clear communication and recognizes that a person needs to have skills to do it. Some four years ago he was introduced to perception checking as part of a university course he was taking. Because he saw this skill as a valuable tool for furthering interstaff effectiveness, he explained it to his co-workers and set aside small portions of their weekly organizational meetings for them to become good at it.

He had his people pair off and sit down face to face. Lou would make a statement regarding her feelings about a new program. Larry would try to reword Lou's sentence. Lou would affirm Larry's interpretation or help him see more clearly what she meant. At times it would take quite a lot of discussion before clear perception resulted.

Taking turns and practicing with each of the staff members over the course of several months made its mark. It soon became very natural for them to use the tool they had "purchased" and put to use:

What I hear you saying is that we need to select the coaches of our athletic teams with more care.

Fred, I think you misunderstood what Kathryn was driving at. What I heard her say was that she's really unable to handle all the VBS teacher training by herself.

Sounds to me like the motion that Mr. Watson would really like to make is that we have a special theme for this year's every member visitation and that we have at least two training sessions for our visitors to equip them for working the theme.

And You Can Pursue Listening Skills

Becoming good at reflective listening is a great asset for a church worker. It's especially helpful when someone has begun to express some strong feelings and needs to be heard out. It asks the listener to be a mirror. Reflecting what is heard keeps the speaker talking. A further response can be elicited by simply waiting or nodding or using an "Uh-huh." The listener works hard to hear the feeling and to validate it: "You're really frustrated." "Sounds like you are very disappointed." "The old gal hit you below the belt." A reasonably close reflection will do the trick. It does wonders for an upset family member who then knows that somebody cares. It's much more valuable than any number of communication closers that say that the speaker has no right to strong feelings or that indicate the listener doesn't know what those feelings are.

A series of training sessions may be very much in order for church staff members who are not skilled in decoding the feelings of others or not able to express their own. These skills can be taught, and the staff can learn them, but a teacher may need to be found, and time will be needed for instruction and practice. Real-life practice can take it from there and greatly enhance a person's effectiveness in dealing with people.

Other examples of contrive-and-pursue activities that might be used either to counteract staff relational difficulties or to enhance staff attitudes and skills are the following: (1) determining ways of reducing competition, (2) selecting values clarification strategies for church staff use, (3) improving Bible study skills together, (4) becoming better at reading body language, (5) understanding how team teaching situations work best, (6) discussing the wise use of praise, (7) learning more about group dynamics. However, the items that a staff itself chooses will likely provide the most fruitful pursuits.

We now shift to the selected illustrations that demonstrate the alert and caring staff as it picks up on and capitalizes on what is taking place. The staff that has a will to weld its relational connections can count on special results.

You Can Count on More Collaboration and Coherence

Because Dave had been trained in the use of a problem-solving process, he offered to lead a miniworkshop for his fellow staffers at Shepherd of the Valley. He was certain that the eight steps involved could be used not only to bring a rather complete set of thoughts regarding a problem systematically to the surface, but also to organize and plan suitable solutions. His proposal was accepted. It would be a good way to support Dave and to get the staff together for growth and fellowship. So it was done, and the by-products for this church staff have been in ample evidence.

Dave did such a good job that his colleagues invited him to moderate six portions of committee meetings and studies around the church during the past year. They have drawn on his expertise to provide an impartial and fresh new voice and approach to their tasks.

It has been good for Dave to share his skill. Preparing for a problem-solving session with a co-worker has served to bring the staff together. The collaboration has been helpful. Dave has grown to appreciate more fully what other staffers are currently doing, and he has never failed to gain some important new ideas. He has also marveled at how similar he and his colleagues are in their unity of purpose, and he can see that the closer they grow in their relationships, the more they trust one another, and the more coherent they become. Like a good argument, they seem to be logically consistent and connected. He has enjoyed these recent months at Shepherd of the Valley more than ever.

You Can Count on Increased and Improved Communication

Trinity's pastor, director of Christian education, and deaconess had not been meeting for a daily morning devotion until they were invited by Trinity's principal to join the faculty down at the library every morning at ten till eight. During the two years since then, the three nonschool members of the church staff have grown closer to their colleagues in the school.

Taking turns in presenting five-to-seven-minute devotions has worked well. The devotions have been practical and interesting. The thoughts have usually centered on the church year, often preparing the participants for the Sunday service by focusing on the Scripture readings coming up. The diversity of the staff has brought in quite a variety of devotional elements. The group sings, handles circle prayers comfortably, and often uses a new litany created by the devotion leader of the week.

While these minutes of worship provide rich opportunity for group members to talk to God and hear His voice, the pre- and postworship time also allows staff persons to communicate with each other. Conversing, sharing news, making announcements, teasing, laughing, inquiring, and complimenting are all parts of the coming and going. So much less communication would be taking place were the group not coming together to begin their day.

And the staff members are so much more alert to each other's needs. Sandy's low spirits are signals of impending depression. Kent's curtness indicates that he is under pressure. Trina's watery eyes and nasal voice sound allergy alerts. Al's surprise donut-hole-and-coffee entrance tells the group that he has a special spiritual victory to share. Communication has gone beyond words. Clothing and hair can speak. An absence may be an outcry. Tardiness could be a sign that overstress is underway. A regular daily opportunity to be together for several punctual, purposeful, and peaceful minutes has strengthened staff member communications immensely for the troops at Trinity.

You Can Count on Growth in Self-Esteem

A person-oriented staff is something most churches want and believe they have in place. It's vital to the whole matter of ministry. The church is people. Yet far too often, church professionals pay little attention to the estimates their fellow workers have of themselves. They fail to appreciate the importance of feeling good about one's personhood. It has little to do with self-centeredness if an individual has a strong self-respect; it's quite the opposite. It has little to do with humility if someone has a low self-image and puts himself down easily and often. Self-esteem has a lot to do with being satisfied and comfortable with who one is. It has a lot to do with wholeness and happiness.

The wise church staff takes time to talk about the importance of self-esteem in people's lives. It even dares to deal with the question in regard to itself. (Yes, the self-esteem of the staff at First Presbyterian may be considerably higher than that at Hoboken Heights Reformed.) Does it make a difference? Of course. Can something be done about it? Certainly. The staff that wants to raise its self-estimate will also dare to deal with the fact that it is made up of individuals who each have a certain level of self-respect, a level that can be raised or lowered as they go about their everyday tasks.

A pastor can have all the outward appearances of a well-adjusted, content, able person, but still be dealing with great insecurities. We all know that he's regularly receiving evaluative comments and that there is no shortage of high expectations, but who bothers to build him up as a person? Who are his ministers? Certainly his fellow staff members can be people who get close enough to him to know his fears, accept his shortcomings, and care about his growth as a person. How sad it is when the church worker with a weak view of himself is not built up in appropriate ways. He may use inappropriate ways that are often based on a tangled and confused picture of who he really is and what he can do about it. Neither alcoholism nor divorce are strangers among today's clergy. A deep problem has a deep connection with how one views himself.

Severe psychological problems require professional attention. A serious case of depression won't be cured by a staffmate's comments, calls, or cards. Those acts will, however, be some of the little things that can hold big pieces together while a person goes through a hospitalization, a series of counseling sessions, or other professional assistance. While each takes extra thought and extra minutes, the time is invested wisely if it serves to build another's self-image. The following suggestions are examples that work. Occasionally an attempt to build someone else up will backfire, but the acceptance and valuing that one is trying to communicate in these genuine and caring ways is likely to bloom over the course of time. (Your own parallel list will work just as nicely. You've heard it somewhere before: It's the thought that counts.)

Ten Ways to Prize My Co-worker

1. Drop by her office, his classroom, her desk, or their house just to say hello. Have no other purpose than that you wish to demonstrate that you value this person.
2. Mail a birthday card. Make sure you write at least four or five personal sentences that focus on the recipient as a valued individual.
3. Include her in your prayers. Schedule a staff person a day on your calendar for a thoughtful, deep prayer. Mention co-workers by name in prayers that begin or close a committee meeting that touches their work.
4. Invite him out to lunch. Have her family over to your house for supper. Don't bowl anyone over with your choices of menu. Treat them the way you think they'd like to be treated. Pray an ex corde prayer that includes thanks for your fellow minister.
5. Use your sense of humor. You can tease some people, and they love it. You can cut out cartoons for others. Share funny stories with those who enjoy funny stories and who will enjoy passing them on to others.
6. Ask your co-worker to do something to help you. Make it manageable, even easy, but never make it artificial. She's doing you a favor. It'll be good for her to give. Leave a special note of thanks on her desk.

7. Honor your colleague's mother and father when you get the opportunity. Saying a special word of thanks for their giving a child to the church would be nice. Do it with a letter or say it to them when they visit. If they are in town for a vacation, you can have them over or arrange some time to take them sight-seeing.
8. Keep tabs on the children of your co-workers. Know their names, what they do, and what is happening that may be special. Have your spouse help you know and value the other spouses.
9. Know what your fellow staffer plays—a cello, backgammon, pinochle, hockey, racquetball. Perhaps you can play together on occasion. Maybe you can teach him how to throw a horseshoe or play cribbage.
10. Take care of his garden and water her plants while they are on vacation.

Giving of oneself through creative boosts to another's self-esteem is a personal act. It reaches out as God is constantly reaching out. It prizes the co-worker. It says, "You count!" And the blessings will follow. The relationship will grow. So it is, too, whenever one brother proclaims the Gospel to another. It is a personal, loving act that says, "I prize you. I count you worthy of hearing that God loves you. I care enough about you to risk embarrassment. I'll tell you the simple facts of God's total acceptance in Jesus, your Savior."

You Can Count on Repentance and Forgiveness

As the workers in Christian ministry carry on their professional tasks in the church, they are a modeling microcosm of the body of Christ in action. They'll put time into being a fellowship of repentant and forgiven sinners. When problems arise in relationships, their Spirit-led response will point them to the sin that continues to be a part of their lives and that keeps on fighting against oneness and mutual respect and love. Repentance is the death of sin. It suffocates and rids. The sin is seen, and the sinner also sees that he has succumbed to it and couldn't pull away from its hold. Sorrow floods in and fills the mind and heart of this person of God.

I wish I hadn't said that. It slipped out. I'm sorry.

It makes me feel so rotten to say so, but for some reason I lied to you yesterday. I feel awful that I did it, and it bugs me that I couldn't admit it right away.

I'm really unhappy that I got so angry. I blew it, and it bothers me plenty to have been so unloving. I'm not proud of it one bit.

And the forgiveness is at hand. The saddened brother enacts the apostle Paul's direction in Romans 6:11 and counts himself "dead to sin," and his fellow minister communicates forgiveness. No time is to be lost. No bigger priority dare stand in the way. It is felt and said quickly and in a sincere, convincing way. The raising-again forgiveness happens just as Paul's sentence in Romans continues: "but alive to God in Christ Jesus."

The church staff is a community of the dead and risen in Christ. They're people that can reach deeply into themselves. They can risk a marvelous ideal such as the one that Paul describes as "speaking the truth in love" (Eph. 4:15). It's a group that can risk honest togetherness. They can open the door to their hearts and unseal their lips. They know that living out the forgiveness of God will readily and repeatedly transform their team of kingdom workers into the mature, responsible, loving body of Christ.

It All Comes Together at the Annual Staff Retreat

An outstanding tool for the betterment of staff relationships is a well-planned large package of time away from home. The team will do many of the same things it does ordinarily. It will work hard with a program of study or planning. It will play hard during its recreation periods. Bible study and prayer and special worship opportunities will be of prime importance, even as they are throughout the year, but being in a different setting and using different approaches will provide freshness and foster renewal.

A retreat allows the team to slow down and back up and look at itself. Staff members will have opportunities to enjoy each other and to recognize again how much the team is like a family. Each will grow closer to his fellow worker. Each is likely to strengthen his commitment to ministry, to the congregation, and to the Lord.

To help capture the flavor of an actual retreat we'll share a compilation of evaluation form comments made after an August preschool retreat of the combined staffs of four congregations and the interparish school that they sponsor. With many husbands and wives of staff people also able to be present, the group numbered just over 40.

> The Bible study was great again this year. Covering Colossians as a package gave me a lot of new insights. I enjoyed working in clusters as well as in a full group. Pastor Walsh really helps the Scriptures come alive, and his exegetical know-how is helping all of us become better students of the Bible. It was kind of neat to have everyone using the same version this year.

> Rich did an excellent job of reminding us of all that goes into Christian worship. I was amazed at how quickly his four two-hour blocks sped by. It was good to have a nonstaff person serve in this way. Gives us fresh input. Super to have a topic leader who is so quick-witted and funny.

> Our worship slots were outstanding this year. Good variety. Cal having his morning devotion down at the lake was a real plus. It was nice to see

so many staff people involved. Marcy obviously enjoyed leading the meal prayers, and we all are bound to use some of her choices and approaches in the year ahead. The closing service was an excellent wrap-up. Having communion in the round drew us all together nicely. I think we could improve on our selection of hymns and songs. One of our music people needs to do some advance planning so that we have a nice balance here.

The place was a pretty fair choice. Good to be two hours away from the city. No one was tempted to slip home on either evening. Menu was plenty satisfactory, and the quantity was no problem. It really helps that this retreat center has air conditioning. Sleeping was much better than last year at Camp Walden. The general meeting room was a little cramped. Maybe we could use the chapel more. The grounds around the center are attractive. Lots of people went for walks in their free time. I'd suggest we come back again next August. Having us all go into Danforth for pizza on Wednesday evening was a great idea. Rob did his usual fantastic best at the piano, and everyone really got into the singing. Was a perfect place for Roger to sing his annual song.

Glad to see so many of the spouses make it this year. Wished we could get all of them to try to juggle a couple vacation days to make it work. Ends up being a bit of a marriage enrichment time. Our singles seemed to all fit in nicely. Have any of them thought about bringing a special friend? Could work.

Having a fairly structured schedule really helps, and I'm glad that Vern keeps us on it, too. The recreation choices were very good, although the time blocks were a little tight. Showers take time. Let's stick with a 3:00 p.m. Tuesday starting time to a 1:00 p.m. Thursday closing time. Seemed like three days, but was really more like two.

Was really helpful to once again spend time on our upcoming year's theme. It will mean so much, much more to us all. Was good to review the goals we wrote last May. Also was good to buzz through the calendar for the whole school year. The advance planning we do here is great.

A wide range of bonding experiences is made possible when a staff goes on a retreat. Many are contrived and pursued. The topic was carefully selected and suited the group well. They had not explored worship together as deeply as this. It was not an accident that the group ended up going out for pizza at a place with a piano.

On the other hand, many of the experiences simply happened. People saw opportunities and capitalized on them. The Spirit was present and provided much more blessing than ever could have been planned. A retreat planned in the name of the Lord for a set of His workers is well worth the time it takes.

Time is a special commodity, and it is to be managed for ministry. God wants our hours to be used in doing His kinds of activities. Coveting packages of time for use in relationship building is basic to His kind of work. Koinonia was His idea. It is His gift to all who gather in His name to live in His ways. And wanting the time for strengthening His family's kinship comes first.

Next, we must corral that time. That, too, will take the necessary desire to do so, but it also takes ideas and administrative skills. We hope this chapter has motivated the reader to reach for both and to do so with wisdom and care.

Managing time properly is the stewardship that makes the difference. It is not difficult for most church staff people to use up all the time available to them. It is not uncommon to find them putting in much extra time and still be plugging away at the same day's regular workload. Much of that time will be meaningful, but it may not be watering the garden of staff relationships as well as it could. The caring and wise church staff will change that. It will start with calendars in hand.

6
Using Time Effectively to Get the Job Done

TEAM MINISTRY EXISTS to further effective ministry in the local parish. Picturing what the team could one day be like certainly includes building harmonious relationships and taking the necessary time to improve those relationships. But equally important, the team needs to use time effectively to get the job done. Sometimes members of a church staff get along well and enjoy each other's company, but very little seems to be happening to equip God's people for carrying out the Great Commission.

This chapter follows up on the section in chapter one on effective ministry and the discussion in chapter two on responsible and accountable leadership. It provides specific and practical help for working together as a team to get the job done. Much of the practical help for improving relationships in the previous chapter, including suggestions for a staff retreat, serves as background for what follows. First, we discuss the importance of personal preparation for an effective team ministry. Then we highlight purposes for meeting times and time-saving meeting procedures. Finally, we will stress the importance of a team-oriented facility. God has showered us with His blessings of eternal life through Jesus Christ, the power of His life-giving Word, a variety of gifts and talents within the local expression of His body, and priceless opportunities for outreach to a dying world. What better response can we give to His gracious love than the spiritual worship of practical, effective ministry each day?

Personal Preparation Time

Jack Jones, the director of Christian education at Emanuel Church, comes to the regular Monday morning staff meeting at the end of August with great enthusiasm. He says to Pastor Edward, "I'm tremendously excited about my Bible class program for the fall. We start the Sunday after Labor Day, and I have found excellent material on the Christian family. I'm hoping you will teach one class, and I've lined up two or three laypersons to lead classes during the week. I plan to give our secretary the whole program to type up tomorrow and would like time on the agenda at the September board meeting to encourage our members to participate. Would you be willing to plug this program in your sermons for the next few weeks?"

Pastor Edward greets Jack's enthusiasm with silence for a moment and then replies in a measured tone of voice, "Jack, I can tell you are enthused, but why didn't you tell me about your plans before now? Didn't you know we were planning to make a strong evangelism effort this fall to prepare for my adult instruction class that begins the last week in September? I'm busy mobilizing our lay leaders to help make calls. I'm hoping you will make calls also. I want to stress witnessing in my sermons and Bible class for September. I'm not against the Christian family, but I don't want too many emphases at the same time. If you want to have a class during the week, I wouldn't object. By the way, my secretary will be rather busy this week updating our evangelism prospect list. I don't know if she can work in your program or not."

Jack feels the wind rushing out of his sails. He has already ordered the Bible class materials and was depending on the pastor's cooperation. He had already talked to some of the board of education members and had them enthused. His plan had seemed so workable and worthwhile. Now his hard work appeared fruitless. The pastor didn't understand. Jack felt betrayed and powerless. He couldn't even make use of the secretary when he needed her assistance.

Pastor Edward felt slightly irked. Couldn't Jack see the importance of evangelism in the congregation? He shouldn't expect to run the whole parish when his education plans spilled over into other areas. The secretary was available to him, but not at his whim. Pastor Edward hoped that Jack was learning a lesson. Yet he didn't want to discourage Jack's initiative.

Does this example sound familiar? Both director of Christian education and pastor want to do their jobs effectively. Both desire to stress an important area of the church's life. Both feel that they are working in the areas of their particular responsibilities. Both have been involving lay members in their projects. But instead of effective ministry, trouble brews on the horizon. Programs clash in a single time frame. Goals diverge. Secretarial time stands in dispute. Feelings are hurt. Team relationships tear slightly. Discouragement sets in, especially for Jack Jones. How could this conflict have been avoided? Is there a better route to effective ministry?

If a team uses time effectively to get the job done, each staff member will start with personal preparation time. That preparation time includes a clear understanding of his/her job in relationship to that of others.

Understanding Your Job in Relationship

Jack knows that his area of responsibility embraces Christian education. Pastor Edward realizes that he is the staff person in charge of evangelism. Perhaps neither is viewing his job in relationship to the other. Probably Pastor Edward has ultimate administrative responsibility for the parish. Jack should have recognized that a particular educational program involving the total congregation would have to be cleared with Pastor Edward as well as with lay leaders on the board of education. This was particularly true because Jack hoped to use Pastor Edward's Bible class and sermon time for his program. Jack had every right to develop an educational emphasis on the Christian family and to use his special expertise in selecting curricular materials. Even his motivating of lay leaders to support, lead, and participate was excellent. However, the two of them together should have planned the timing and positioning of the program in the total parish ministry well in advance.

Pastor Edward, on the other hand, was responsible for evangelism and was justified in planning a September emphasis, but he failed to ask Jack how the evangelism emphasis would relate to Jack's fall educational plans. In fact, Pastor Edward should have taken the initiative to explore ways that an evangelism emphasis might fit into the educational program during September. Furthermore, as the one responsible for Jack's educational ministry, he should have been encouraging Jack's initiative by planning well in advance to consider Jack's ideas in the light of his own directions for the parish. Then he could have supported Jack's fine program at a later date, and Jack could have provided willing and creative assistance with the evangelism effort. Instead Pastor Edward demotivated Jack and discouraged his initiative.

Understanding your job as it relates to others is a key to effective ministry. What is your relationship to the other staff members, to lay leaders, to boards and committees, to the congregation as a whole? In what areas can you take the initiative and proceed with action steps? When do you need formal approval, informal consultation, communicating, or coordination? In what ways can you encourage and support other staff members in their projects? In what ways can you gain priority consideration for your programs as a contribution to the common good?

In reality we are talking about the management of exchanges. What do I have of value that will meet your needs? What do you have of value that will meet the needs of my particular ministry? How can we share what we have to meet the overall needs of our parish? My primary need may be your secondary need and vice versa. Instead of competing between evangelism and education, we can cooperate in a ministry that embraces both dimensions. If we take the time for personal preparation to understand our job in relation to others' ministries, we will get the work done to God's glory and for the Christian growth of the parish. We also need the personal preparation of utilizing the secretarial staff.

Utilizing the Secretarial Staff

Jack Jones also had a conflict with Pastor Edward over the use of the secretary's time. While Jack needed her to type up his Christian family program for the fall, Pastor Edward needed her to prepare a list of evangelism prospects for the September calling effort. Both had worthwhile projects. Both needed the work to be done soon. Both technically were entitled to use secretarial help for their areas of ministry. The secretary may have felt torn between the conflicting demands on her time.

Whatever your team ministry relationship, secretarial help probably enters into the picture. You may be part of a large parish where two or more full-time secretaries are employed. Perhaps one is designated as the church secretary and one as the school secretary. Perhaps one is designated as the typist-receptionist and the other as the project secretary. Each secretary may service several staff members—a principal and teaching staff or two pastors and a director of Christian education. Questions inevitably arise. For whom does the secretary work? Is she a parish secretary or a pastor's private secretary? Is one staff member in charge of the secretary while other staff members work through the one in charge, or do all staff members equally share the use of secretarial time and assign work as needed? How much work should the secretary do for lay leaders who come in with projects?

You may also be part of a staff where volunteer secretaries are used or where a combination of employed and part-time volunteer secretaries work side by side. Again the questions include who is in charge of what workers. Does one secretary run the office, or does some staff member control the distribution of work? Secretarial assistance can be the source of tensions in team ministry.

Different arrangements are both acceptable and workable, but certain principles are vital to effective utilization of a secretarial staff. Clear lines of responsibility and accountability for the secretarial staff need to be established when a secretary is hired or begins service. A written job description is very helpful. The secretary needs to know what is expected and how the job relates to other staff members. The professional team members need to know how much use each of them can expect to make of secretarial help and what procedures they should follow in assigning work. The congregation and lay leaders also need to know what responsibilities the secretaries have in relation to general parish work. That is why job descriptions, properly approved by the appropriate boards and communicated to the congregation, play such a vital role.

In addition to clear lines of accountability, ongoing communication is also vital. Professional and secretarial staff need to keep in close contact. Secretaries need to share their concerns regarding work load and efficient operation. Professional team members must keep each other informed about special projects that require large amounts of secretarial time. Efficient scheduling can bring about satisfaction and effective work for all parties concerned. Jack's needs and Pastor Edward's projects could both be handled with proper scheduling. Volunteer help could have been brought in to type or to compile the prospect list. Personal preparation includes efficient utilization of the secretarial staff. It also means the setting of mutual deadlines.

Establishing Mutual Deadlines

Every effective worker sets deadlines for the projects at hand. When a pastor serves alone in a parish, he can plan the work according to his own pace and purpose. Even in this instance, if he expects considerable lay involvement, he will need to take the schedules and deadlines of others into account when he carries out his ministry. But if a parish has a professional staff, each team member certainly needs to consider mutual deadlines when planning.

Jack Jones should not have waited until the end of August to bring up a September Christian education emphasis. Even though he was following his own deadlines for ordering curricular materials and lining up lay leaders, he was not considering Pastor Edward's deadlines for an evangelism emphasis. Similarly, Pastor Edward had failed to consider Jack's need to have adequate time for structuring a Christian education program. If the pastor had discussed a parishwide emphasis with Jack in the spring or early summer, they could have developed mutual deadlines agreeable to each. Lay involvement, curriculum integration, a unified publicity effort, and utilization of secretarial time could also have been coordinated with mutual deadlines.

Personal preparation by each staff member involves taking the time to think through ministry plans in his/her area of responsibility in the light of the other ministry areas. Adequate time then will be allowed for unifying the total parish plans, arranging mutual deadlines, and getting the necessary assistance and support for each project.

The first step toward using time effectively to get the work done revolves around personal preparation by each staff member to understand his/her job in relation to others, to utilize the secretarial staff efficiently, and to establish mutual deadlines for parish work. This personal preparation leads to the kinds of meetings with others that will result in effective ministry. We consider first the purposes for meeting times and then time-saving meeting procedures.

Purposes for Meeting Times

Americans seem to be fascinated with meetings. Every conceivable organization exists and schedules meetings to justify its existence. Many meetings consume large amounts of time and accomplish little. The church likewise features a generous dosage of meetings—ladies' groups, men's groups, youth groups, senior citizen groups, official boards and committees, task forces, ad hoc groups—the list goes on and on. Most professional church workers find themselves enmeshed in a network of meetings that can often exhaust and frustrate. Many times we separate meetings and ministry. There seems to be little relationship between meetings and action.

Sometimes our attitudes toward meetings carry over into staff relationships. We conclude that more will be accomplished if each goes a separate direction and does the Lord's work. Meetings, we suggest to ourselves, will only drain time away from vital ministry to and with people. Consequently days, even weeks, go by without much communication. When these attitudes are practiced, the team can scarcely ever coordinate its efforts for effective ministry.

At the other extreme, some teams meet frequently on a formal or informal basis. Regular staff meetings consume large blocks of time. Coffee breaks from work turn into lengthy discussions about any subject that comes to mind. The team feels good about its relationships, but valuable ministry opportunities are lost because of wasted time. This approach likewise falls far short of getting the job done.

In this section we present four purposes for staff meetings. A single meeting may combine two or more of these purposes, but each is worthy of separate attention and determines the style and outcome of a meeting. Note that this section describes meetings designed to get the job done and does not dwell on gatherings for the purpose of building team relationships. Bible study, prayer, and social gatherings have considerable merit, as described in the previous chapter. Meetings for getting work done may also have the side effect of welding a staff together as it considers common tasks. Prayer and devotions should also be included in these business meetings as a constant reminder of our dependence on God for everything.

Brainstorming

The first type of staff meeting has brainstorming as its purpose. The staff gathers to consider a broad area of ministry, for example, the direction for the church in the next 10 years, a potential building program, evangelism, congregational worship, lay participation, or a host of other topics. In a brainstorming session the freedom to express ideas is of paramount importance. No immediate action is intended. Ideas are shared and recorded in some fashion. Everyone is encouraged and expected to participate. Any idea is acceptable. Later the ideas may be correlated and systematized for further consideration, but in the brainstorming session they are shared in a free-flowing sequence.

Some formal techniques or instruments are available to stimulate brainstorming. The activity can also be successfully carried out without any structure at all. Brainstorming can open up a topic and point to fresh, creative suggestions. It also can generate enthusiam for an important area of ministry and develop ownership on the part of the participants. For this reason it is helpful to have brainstorming meetings with both lay and professional groups, including mixtures of the two groups. When the participants know that a meeting is scheduled for brainstorming and that the results will be compiled for further consideration, they will generally participate enthusiastically and find great satisfaction in the results of the discussion. Frequent brainstorming sessions can be very enlivening. Much positive and effective ministry often results.

Planning

A second type of staff meeting concentrates on planning. Much time needs to be spent by any church team in this activity. Many fine books have been written on planning. Professional and lay leaders together need to plan carefully for ministry.

Long-range strategic planning needs to be carried out by each local parish with a consideration for the central purpose of the church, the needs of the parish and community, the problems or roadblocks facing the church, the opportunities available for ministry, and the resources of people, finances, and facilities present within the congregation. Staff members should guide this long-range planning process by meeting privately and encouraging input from lay members of the church. Only when church leadership considers strategic planning important will the church move ahead clearly on its God-given mission. A retreat setting or a regular process over a period of months can be used for long-range planning.

Annual planning by the church staff has great value for the development of themes and directions for the coming year and for the division of responsibilities among staff members. Principal and teachers frequently use this approach for the upcoming school year. Pastors and other church staff can use it for planning worship and Christian education as well. Again a partnership between lay and professional church leaders is vital. Annual planning calls for clear, measurable, and achievable goals and a strategy for reaching those goals.

Detailed planning also needs to be done on a monthly and weekly basis as the team carries out the specifics of the plans that have been made.

Coordination

A third type of staff meeting accomplishes the purpose of coordinating the ministries being carried out. Each staff member shares goals and plans with the rest. Conflicts can be minimized. Schedules are established that incorporate the different programs. Staff members are able to promote each other's areas to the congregation. Mutual support and encouragement are present. Team members challenge each other to accomplish objectives. The pastor can support the principal in his efforts to get more parents active in the parent-teacher organization. The principal can support the pastor in the major undertaking of building a new church. The director of Christian education can willingly volunteer to make evangelism calls, knowing that the pastor will teach a Bible class on the Christian family later in the year.

All staff members are reminded of the purpose of their local parish and can respond with a desire to carry out the Great Commission. They rejoice in their unique ministries, but they also support one another. They see a unified plan and how they fit into that plan. They pull together as a team, not in separate directions. Coordination and clear communication help. Staff members may not always agree, but they can reach a consensus on how they will proceed. These meetings may be brief, but they are very helpful.

Evaluation

A fourth type of staff meeting is for evaluation. In some respects every meeting includes evaluation as reports are made on completed projects. However, regular meetings for evaluation can be very profitable. The supervising staff member, usually the pastor or principal, should meet with each staff member individually to give that person an opportunity to evaluate his/her performance over the past year in preparation for the general meeting. It is best for the staff member to be guided toward self-evaluation by describing effective and ineffective activities, learning that has taken place, and personal strengths and weaknesses. The staff member can also be asked about items that will be worked on for the coming year. This can serve as preliminary goal-setting for evaluation in the next year. The staff evaluation meeting needs to be positive in nature and include affirmation. The pastor should receive evaluation from the board of elders or other top lay leaders after getting input from his other staff members.

The staff should also meet as a group to evaluate periodically the directions of the parish and the effectiveness of various programs and activities.

This meeting would also produce suggestions for improvement in the future. Lay input should be solicited to improve the evaluation's accuracy. Questionnaires can be used in advance of the meeting to guide discussion.

Staff meetings should be clear in purpose. Brainstorming, planning, coordination, and evaluation are unique purposes that may blend together in a given meeting or be considered at separate meetings. When the participants are clear as to the purpose, the meeting accomplishes a great deal, and the team is unified in a common task. Regardless of the meeting's purpose, there are certain time-saving meeting procedures that we now consider.

Time-Effective Meeting Procedures

A disorganized meeting frustrates all the participants. People come because of duty, pay little attention, disrupt the proceedings, and complain about the results. Yet meetings continue to waste time on a regular basis. This section looks at simple tips for conducting effective meetings.

Before the Meeting

1. Schedule essential meetings on a regular basis. Rather than call a faculty meeting only when needed or convenient, set a monthly or twice-a-month meeting time that everyone can plan on. Otherwise hectic schedules will rob you of necessary meeting time, and communication will deteriorate.

2. Coordinate personal and church calendars when scheduling meetings. You will want to have a calendar in your office that corresponds with one the secretary keeps for you. It should be kept current with any pocket calendar you might carry with you and with any calendar maintained at home. Other staff members would also profit by having coordinated personal calendars. Make sure that all meeting dates are cleared on everyone's calendar when setting up your schedule of meetings. Encourage staff members to bring calendars with them to meetings in case any additional meetings or activities need to be scheduled. Always make sure that future dates are noted at each meeting. Make sure that all meetings are recorded on the church or school calendars in the main office area.

3. Think ahead to maximize the value of each meeting. Use regular meetings as much as possible. Don't waste people's time by unnecessary meetings or by dragging out meetings when little needs to be covered. Make certain that the right people are present at the meetings in which their input is needed. Those in authority and those who have the specialized knowledge required should be present so that they can be involved in the process and contribute what is needed.

4. Prepare specific agendas in advance. The leader needs to get input

from participants and other leaders prior to the meeting so that the necessary items can be considered. Participants should receive a copy of the agenda prior to the meeting so that they can come prepared.

5. Communicate with reports and memos. In addition to using the agenda, the leader can keep individual members in touch with the issues at hand by written memos. This can be especially helpful when certain individuals are given assignments for the meeting, such as devotions or reports. It is also helpful for reports to be prepared in writing. Much time can be saved and much more can be accomplished when each individual making a report prepares in writing a clear summary of the points to be covered. This presentation should be duplicated if possible and given to the other staff members by the meeting time. Formal reports or typed memos are even helpful before a meeting between only two staff members. The discussion will stick more closely to the purpose for the meeting. Jotting down notes before a phone call can also maximize the value of the call.

6. Provide for appropriate facilities. Make certain that a room is reserved that will provide the right atmosphere for the meeting—chairs and tables, adequate lighting, a comfortable temperature, the necessary equipment for audio and visual aids, access to refreshments, if planned, etc. Also make sure that the room is properly set up in advance of the meeting.

During the Meeting

1. Stick to the agenda. It can be reviewed at the beginning of the meeting, and other items can be added as necessary, but it should be strictly followed. Certain items can receive more attention by design. This intention could be indicated by designating the time to be spent on each item.

2. Stick to the time schedule. Meetings should begin promptly and conclude at an agreed time. Prolonging a meeting should only be done with the agreement of the whole group.

3. Provide for helpful interaction. The purpose of the meeting should determine the agenda and format. Although certain procedures may be followed, the important feature is not the mechanics of the meeting but the meaningful interaction of the participants. Keep team building in mind. Give all sides an opportunity to express themselves. The enthusiastic participation of the team members holds the key to effective staff ministry. As the meeting progresses, note the nonverbal cues from the participants. If some are grading papers or reading other material, you know that less than total attention is being given. Restlessness, looking at watches, late arrival, and early departure communicate lack of involvement. Other body language may indicate divisions within the group, attentiveness, intensity, or pulling together on an issue. These cues may provide an opportunity for group reflection on the process

and content of meetings, thus leading to more meaningful and cooperative sessions together.

4. Reach decisions by consensus. The process may take more time, but the results are worth the effort. Different points of view can strengthen the eventual decisions made. Sometimes action will have to be taken without complete agreement. Be careful to affirm the opinions of dissenters and value their insights. Respect the authority of those charged with certain decisions even if you do not agree.

5. Summarize the meeting and clarify assignments at the end. Make sure that no items are still dangling. Resolve the issues and make sure everyone knows who is responsible for carrying them out, or place uncompleted items on the agenda for the next meeting. Don't hesitate to have an individual or small group do additional research and bring recommendations to the next meeting.

After the Meeting

1. Record accurate minutes of the meeting and send copies to all participants. Stress the decisions reached, the assignments made, and the tentative items for the next meeting. Include the time and place for the next meeting.

2. Each participant should make careful note of his/her responsibilities as a result of the meeting and schedule time to carry them out so that a report can be given at the next meeting. Remember that most of the actual work is done between meetings.

The Team-Oriented Facility

Who would dispute that a church building has its work to do and its witness to make? The kind of edifice that it is, its aesthetic qualities, the furniture and equipment it contains, the housekeeping it receives, the arrangement and care given to its offices and rooms are all items that reflect the importance this place has for the nurture of its members' ministry. The environment also cannot avoid making a commentary about the team ministry of the staff that is using the building as its home base. While a discussion of the congregation's plant clearly relates to job effectiveness in terms of everyday work functions, it is necessary to point out that the team orientation of a building or set of buildings also has major ramifications.

We could have easily stressed its importance in chapter three. How clearly does the facility describe teamness to the new staff candidate on his/her first visit? It might also have received special emphasis in chapters one and five, for relationships can be affected greatly by the decisions made about the arrangement of the work place. Jealousy, resentment, and covetousness can be brought on by not considering a team member's space needs or feelings about the building. Snide and cutting remarks will be as permanently installed as walls when a decided lack of interest in team matters is reflected in either a new building project or its remodeling and renovation.

Chapter two could also have incorporated these ideas, for the leadership on the professional staff has major responsibilities to both parish and staff to initiate and carry out a workable and effective, considerate and caring plan of plant usage by the staff team. Excessive attention to the needs of leadership is often at the root of plant problems.

These are far-reaching concerns raised by the questions related to building and equipment utilization. The following analysis of the problem is by no means an exhaustive discussion, but it illustrates the thinking that is present when team consciousness governs decisions regarding church plant planning and management. Head pastors, school principals, and other church administrators should cultivate and adhere to four senses as they include buildings in the business of balancing, blending and bonding the team.

A Sense of Equality

Differences in room size and decor are surely to be expected and prized. An office or a classroom should allow for its main occupant's best qualities to be reflected and enhanced. Wall covering, paint, carpet, and drapery can so easily allow for individual ideas and suggestions. Freedom of choice surely belongs—that is, if it stays within the parameters that exist. And that's where a sense of equality must be exercised in regard to factors like cost, size, number, and team ministry.

Having built-in shelving and cabinetry of wood is just not the same as a freestanding metal bookcase. An executive-style, two-pedestal desk is not comparable to a table. Plush carpeting and tile floors are not equal. The sense of equality does not have to be absolutely precise. Usually it must focus primarily on the dollars expended. Surely there are allowances to be made for positions of responsibility, but these should be kept in healthy and kind perspective. There is simply no need for a head pastor's office to receive budgetary considerations of thousands of dollars when other staff people receive little or none.

Helpful to the cause of equality is the idea that some things can be exactly the same—perhaps the desk chair or the drapes. Quantity purchasing of certain items is not only good stewardship of money; it can go a long way toward creating camaraderie and good will.

A Sense of Teamness

Let's think about typing and printing. These two everyday staff needs can give administrators a lot to consider. Picture the church's nursery school office with its aged Underwood and its hand-crank duplicator and then take a look at the church office's IBM Selectric and its Multilith offset. But don't stop there. Why not "team" them? The two operations may well need to exist, but not in isolation. There is a happy solution awaiting the team that discusses the dreams and realities, the problems and needs. It simply must take the time to team. Sharing and cooperating, giving and getting are just such a part of the everyday functioning of the busy, energetic church staff as it lives within its means and its mode. The sense of teamness will go a long way toward preventing difficulties. It suggests that we think as a team from the beginning. Opportunity for all staff to express their ideas should always be given, and sufficient time should be allowed to study their proposals.

A Sense of the Value of Recognition

Each staff person, from custodian to clergy, has that estimate of self to recognize and regard. The worker who feels good about his work is also going to get it done in better fashion. Putting the new vicar in a cubbyhole with a card table just might take the edge off the excitement he had when he left the seminary and headed your way. Would it not have been better to do some thoughtful preparation of an appropriate spot, have it listed on the building directory at the front door, and install a spiffy new nameplate at his office entrance?

Deliberately thoughtful planning can easily provide the positive regard that builds up a sister or brother on the staff. Each team member ought to view the colleague's place of work as something that she/he can help make a more compatible and happy place. It says, "I care about you as a person," and "We work together."

A Sense of Smooth Functioning

Togetherness is not only a pattern for good feelings about work; it is also a pattern for getting your work done in a smooth way. A team-oriented facility provides the enjoyment of special efficiencies by having its work done together.

How offices and rooms are arranged can cut down a lot of waste in both time and energy. Where supplies are located can be a team-considered matter. Then there is the telephone and all that it means to doing one's work. There is also the smooth scheduling and use of meeting rooms and other spaces in common.

As the staff members model the harmonious and effective team in their everyday functioning, so also the building facility loudly declares that it is a place in which a supportive and caring, cooperative and helpful team leads the way. Team-oriented buildings are parish blessings.

This chapter has focused on the practicality of using time effectively to get the work done. Each staff member needs individual preparation time to understand the job in relation to others, to utilize the secretarial staff efficiently, and to establish mutual deadlines. The individual preparation paves the way for effective meetings, whether for the purpose of brainstorming, planning, coordinating, or evaluating. The meeting's procedures can save time if careful preparation occurs before the meeting, the actual meeting time is used in the best way, and the meeting's follow-up is thorough. The everyday working conditions, including the use of facilities and equipment, require a team orientation. Effective ministry for Christ is the goal of all team relationships.

Conclusion

HOW HAVE YOU FOUND YOUR PLUNGE into the waters of team ministry? You have been testing the depths of harmonious staff relationships and effective ministry for Gospel mission. The words of this book describe the ideal and flirt with the reality of team ministry in today's parishes. You may like the carefully defined Olympic-size swimming pool of this book. The water feels comfortable—just the right temperature. You can follow the markers and enjoy the relaxing swim or choose to swim laps in a disciplined and challenging fashion. You enjoy being part of a swimming team. You work to your individual potential but participate with your team members, supporting and challenging each other to new goals for a common purpose.

Sounds great! But you remain skeptical. "We don't have an Olympic-size swimming pool where I work. It's a gravel pit—no markings or boundaries, no springboards, treacherous footing, uncomfortable temperatures, no lifeguards, no sense of teamwork, everyone out for number one. How can we achieve harmonious relationships and effective ministry when we simply struggle for survival? Members of the parish don't get along with each other. They form competing groups. And they seem to have little sense of Gospel mission beyond keeping the doors open and paying the bills. How can we possibly develop a team ministry and make it work in a gravel pit or a powerful river or a large lake or a turbulent ocean?"

Although skeptical and fearful, you demonstrate keen insight. Your parish *is* unique. Small churches differ from medium and large churches. Rural settings contrast with urban and suburban settings. Parishes with schools have different problems and opportunities than parishes without schools. Congregations feature a unique blend of personalities, history, customs and traditions, social class background, and theological orientation. Professional staff members likewise bring a variety of qualities, skills, and backgrounds to the parish setting. This book needs to become your book with the principles adapted to your parish, your team, and your personality.

Further, you have correctly observed that your team relationships and effectiveness are influenced by the relationships and effectiveness of your parish. A divided and apathetic congregation spells trouble for professional team ministry.

Have you succeeded in neutralizing the impact of this book on your ministry? Do you feel that it's interesting, thought-provoking, and ideal but not written for you or your staff in your parish? Will you simply put it on the shelf and continue swimming around in circles through your bayou trying to avoid alligators and other team members?

You may have keen insights about practical realities in your parish. But have you forgotten Him? Have you forgotten the One who called the church into existence in the first place; the One who came into a world of fractured relationships with a message of healing, acceptance, and forgiveness; the One who took on Himself the alienation and sin of the whole world and paid the full price with His death on the cross; the One who by His death restored relationships—both the vertical and the horizontal? Jesus Christ combined effective ministry with caring relationships in His life, death, and resurrection. This book on team ministry only has meaning and potential because of Him. He deals with skepticism and fear by showing us His nail-pierced hands so that we cry out in joyful confession: "My Lord and my God!"

Jesus Christ also has called your parish into existence. As you regularly gather around the Word and Sacraments, the risen Lord builds caring relationships among members who reach out to one another with His love. And He likewise empowers and directs your parish members into effective Gospel ministry in word and deed. The sharp message of the Law exposes selfishness, indifference, and division. The comforting message of the Gospel brings unity, cooperation, and zeal for mission.

Jesus Christ has also brought your professional team together with a common purpose. He alone can build harmonious relationships and enable effective ministry. That's what this book is all about—letting Him work in you to develop and sustain team ministry. Clear expectations, solid spiritual foundation, authority to lead, ability to lead, serving, accepting responsibility to lead, recognizing accountability to others, teamwork knowledge, team skills, teamwork habits, team attitudes, knowing yourself, improving relationships by listening and caring, working at team communication, retreat time together, getting the job done together, effective meetings, team-oriented facilities, job descriptions—all are ways of bringing the Gospel to bear on professional staff members working together on His mission while growing closer to each other and to Jesus Christ.

Your team, empowered and directed by God in Christ, becomes a model in the parish for harmonious relationships and effective ministry. Working together, supporting each other, urgently sharing the Gospel, caring for others, admitting mistakes and confessing sins, forgiving and giving, your team's example catches on contagiously and infectiously. God grips the parish through you so that the Word comes alive in ministry. The whole parish operates as His team for the community and for the world.

God receives the glory. His Kingdom comes. His will is done through you, your professional team, and the whole parish. A skeptical you, a tottering professional team, and a divided apathetic parish are transformed into a mighty, growing team engaged in His mission. Perhaps this book will provide for you a small beginning, a fresh start, a practical handle, a Gospel hope. The stakes are high; the potential is great; and the blessings are abundant for developing a professional team ministry and making it work. Now is clearly the time to team—for God's glory!

Appendix A
Sample Job
Descriptions

Large Congregation with a School

(The following three samples illustrate the approach of a large congregation with a school to a pastoral staff of three.)

Job Description: Senior Pastor—Administration

I. We authorize and obligate our senior pastor to be responsible for the following areas of the total program of our church:

A. Coordination and Administration

1. Assist boards, committees, and organizations with counsel and leadership.

a. Boards: Council, Trustees, Education

b. Committees: Stewardship, Proportionate Giving, Talent Enlistment, Sponsor, Evangelism, Elders, Executive, Finance, Church Foundation, Nominating, Constitution, Scholarship, Archives, Public Relations, Tracts, Social Welfare, Ushers, Parish Planning Program, Salary Study

c. Organizations: Ladies Aid, Mission Guild, Married Couples Club, Nursery, Altar Guild, Fisherman Club, 70 and Out Couples Clubs, Vineyard Club

d. Any other boards, committees, and organizations that may be created

2. Call meetings of pastors and teachers to coordinate plans, programs, and mission of the church.

3. Receive reports of all committees, boards, and organizations within the church to assist him in the supervision of the church's program.

4. Supervise school staff members who have certain responsibilities delegated to them beyond their duties specifically connected with the school, such as playing the organ, directing the choir, parish planning, Bible class, Sunday school, etc.

5. Offer training programs in leadership two times a year—in January for congregational leaders and in May for leaders of organizations.

B. Worship
   1. Develop the worship program—themes, types of services, advance planning, music, preachers, liturgists, etc.
   2. Preach twice as often as the associate pastor.
   3. Conduct weddings and funerals by request and reference. Baptisms will be conducted by the liturgist except when a teacher is the liturgist.
C. New Members
   The senior pastor is responsible for those coming into the church by transfer, affirmation of faith, or adult confirmation. The program for receiving new members involves the following: an office visit; a home visit; receiving of a Talent Enlistment Form, a personal record form, and a pledge form; giving them tracts, devotion guides, a calendar back, *Witness*, a picture directory, envelopes, etc.; seeing that they are welcomed in worship service; having their picture taken and posted; enlisting them in some way in the life of the parish; seeing that they receive a phone call and letter. One year from the date of acceptance, the new members will be referred either to the elders as active, integrated members or to the Evangelism Committee as delinquent.
D. Teaching
   1. Plan, teach, and supervise adult classes for new members.
   2. Share in the teaching of children's confirmation classes.
   3. Teach the Bethel Bible Series to congregational leaders.
   4. Share in the Bible class teaching.
E. Counseling (by request and reference)
F. Calling
   1. Hospital and shut-in calls only by request from the pastor to families.
   2. Prospective membership calls.
   3. Special problem calls.
G. Larger Church Service (Circuit, District, Synod, Community)
   As the need arises and as the congregation will allow.
H. Community Ministry
   Foster a cooperative spirit with interdenominational and community programs.
 I. Professional Growth
   Attend conferences, seminars, and workshops for keeping abreast of the administrative ministry and continued growth.
II. We authorize and obligate our senior pastor to observe and maintain the following relationships:
   A. Meet with the associate pastors weekly and receive reports in order to plan and coordinate goals, programs, and schedules of the ministry to families, the ministry to youth, and the work with the boards, committees, and organizations of the congregation.
   B. Meet weekly with the principal to receive information concerning the school and to share items of interest concerning the larger picture of the total ministry in the congregation.

Job Description: Associate Pastor—Pastor to Families

 I. We authorize and obligate our pastor to families to carry out the following responsibilities:
   A. Visitation
      1. Visit all the members in their homes on a regular and continual basis.

      2. Assume the primary responsibility for calling on the sick, the hospitalized, and the shut-ins.

  B. Boards and Committees

      1. Provide for training, guiding, and working with

        a. the Board of Elders;

        b. the associate elders;

        c. the visitation committees.

      2. Maintain, with the aid of the above boards and committees, an effective personal ministry that will help every family of the congregation to become a spiritually growing, responsible Christian family unit.

  C. Worship

      1. Share in the preaching on the average of one time for every two times that the senior pastor preaches.

      2. Conduct weddings, funerals, and other services by request and reference.

  D. Existing Members (those who have been members for more than one year)

      1. Maintain a personal record of every family.

      2. Supervise all correspondence in regard to membership changes, status, and referrals.

      3. Assume the primary responsibility in dealing with family crisis situations in the congregation.

      4. Deal with the delinquents and other problem cases of the congregation with the Board of Elders.

  E. Teaching

      1. Share in teaching junior and adult confirmation classes.

      2. Conduct seminars and workshops that will help to establish more meaningful family relationships.

      3. Teach the Bethel Bible Series to associate elders.

      4. Share in the Bible class teaching.

  F. Counseling (by request and reference)

  G. Larger Church Service (Circuit, District, Synod, Community)

    As the need arises and as the congregation will allow.

  H. Professional Growth

    Attend conferences, seminars, and workshops for keeping abreast of family ministry and continued growth.

II. We authorize and obligate our pastor to families to observe and maintain the following relationships:

  A. Meet regularly with the other pastors for support and guidance and for planning and coordinating family goals, programs, and schedules with those of the rest of the parish.

  B. Attend the Church Council and voters' meetings and periodically share with them the program of the ministry to families.

Job Description: Associate Pastor—Pastor to Youth

I. We authorize and obligate our pastor to youth to carry out the following responsibilities:

  A. Guide the youth of our church in knowing, living, and sharing the forgiving Christ and in active participation in the life of the church.

  B. Study the congregation and the community to determine the youth picture and how the church can best meet the needs of our young people.

C. Be a friend "in Christ" and a counselor to youth.

D. Keep a personal record of every youth.

E. Make personal contact with each young person in the congregation through interviews, cell discussion groups, youth retreats, and home visitations.

F. Keep in touch with youth at college and in the military and serve as pastoral adviser to the Armed Services Committee.

G. Be pastoral adviser to the single adult organization and the Vineyard Club.

H. Assist the youth counselors in aiding the youth groups by planning and carrying out stimulating and active programs of Christ-centered education and service.

I. Train youth to assume leadership responsibility.

J. Coordinate the youth program with the life of the congregation.

K. Develop, coordinate, and supervise meaningful activities for the youth that center in the youth room and gymnasium.

L. Preach approximately once a month, except during Lent and Advent. There would be additional opportunities to preach at special youth services.

M. Encourage and train youth to participate in the worship, evangelism, service, and education programs in the church.

N. Emphasize participation in Bible study classes, Christ-centered discussion groups, worship, and Holy Communion, and foster and promote person-to-person concern "in Christ" for newcomers to our community.

O. Reactivate the inactive youth and bring the Gospel message to unchurched youth in the high school as well as to individuals in the community.

P. Assist in the teaching program of the church, such as the training of youth Bible class teachers and working with teachers in confirmation instruction.

Q. Arrange for youth fellowship through attendance at rallies, camps, conventions, workshops, and outings.

R. Cooperate with families of young people in carrying out their responsibilities and gaining insight into the perspectives of youth.

S. Involve parents in assisting with the youth program.

T. Enlist and train youth counselors.

U. Make home visitations on all families of youth and minister to them in times of crises.

V. Make hospital calls when youth are admitted and assume responsibility for visiting all other members in that hospital at that time.

W. Keep youth work before the members of the church through reports to voters' meetings, etc.

X. Keep abreast of the work of the church and be able to show the relevance of youth work to the church.

Y. Strive for continual professional growth.

Z. Develop a youth library of books and magazines for the youth, the counselors, and the pastor to youth.

AA. Meet regularly with the other pastors for support and guidance and share mutually the youth work of the congregation.

II. We authorize and obligate our pastor to youth to observe and maintain the following relationships:

A. Senior Pastor

1. Plan and coordinate youth goals, programs, schedules, and especially any innovations with those of the parish.

2. Plan with him the projected preaching and worship schedule.

B. Pastor to Families
  1. Keep him informed concerning families visited so that the Associate Elder Program can be directed more effectively.
  2. Receive hospital assignments from him and report on all visits made.
C. Congregation
  Be responsible directly to the Board of Education for the youth program and serve as a resource person to the board in the execution of its responsibilities for youth.
D. Youth Counselors
  Train lay people to share responsibility for youth programming and serve as a resource person to them.
E. Parents
  Cooperate with the parents in their primary responsibility for the Christian growth of their young people.
F. Youth
  Establish a personal relationship of love and concern in Christ for each youth in the congregation. The primary responsibility will be to the youth from seventh grade to marriage.

Medium-Sized Congregation Without a School

(The following three samples illustrate the approach of a medium-sized congregation without a school to its pastor, director of Christian education, and youth minister.)

Job Description: Senior Pastor

I. Job Summary
  The senior pastor shall be the overseer of the congregation. He stands at the head of his congregation as one who is charged with the duty of caring for the church of God. In a congregation that recognizes the Biblical concept of the priesthood of all believers and earnestly strives to make a living reality of that fact that "everyone is a minister," it becomes a New Testament challenge to serve as the called undershepherd of the flock.
II. Work Required
  A. The senior pastor shall regularly feed the flock by
    1. Preaching at worship services (Sunday morning and special services)
      a. Pulpit absences may include four Sundays yearly for vacation; two to four Sundays yearly for National Guard duties (an extended exception may be granted by the Board of Lay Ministry); and up to eight Sundays per year to lead retreats, conferences, etc., for other congregations and groups.
      b. Occasional guest speakers may preach when the senior pastor is present when it is deemed beneficial and advisable for the congregation by the Board of Lay Ministry.
    2. Administering the Sacraments
      a. Baptism
        1) Instructing parents and sponsors of children and individual adult candidates for Baptism in the Biblical understanding of Baptism.
        2) Responsibly administering Baptism both in worship situations and in private services for the congregation.

    b. Holy Communion
       1) Instructing those wishing to partake of the Eucharist and encouraging frequent participation by all who are instructed.
       2) Consecrating or supervising the consecration of the elements for distribution of the Sacrament within the congregation.
       3) Training the lay ministers and other assistants in the proper distribution of the Sacrament and also in how to instruct those who wish to partake of the Eucharist with the church.

3. Leading Worship
    a. Planning and preparing suitable orders of worship for use in the services of the congregation. Such services are to include regular worship and special services (wedding, funeral, private baptism, house blessings, etc.)
    b. Leading or supervising the leading of worship, including the music portions of the services.

4. Teaching the Word
    a. Serving as the principal instructor for junior and adult confirmation classes.
    b. Teaching Bible-based courses, especially on an adult level, for spiritual growth among congregational members.
    c. Equipping the saints for ministry with specific training, including evangelism activities and youth ministry.
    d. Instructing the lay ministers to assist in the shepherding of the flock.
    e. Leading congregational retreats and classes for renewal.
    f. Leading a home Bible study group when possible and encouraging discipleship training in small group settings.

B. The senior pastor shall oversee the flock by
  1. Guiding the direction and growth of the congregation.
    a. Sharing formally in teaching and growth sessions with all congregational members.
    b. Attending Planning Council meetings and participating in its work by sharing visions, challenges, and encouragement.
    c. Attending the various board meetings when possible and desirable or sharing with the boards through other means of communication in order to encourage, support, and strengthen the ongoing work of the church.
    d. Giving doctrinal supervision to all aspects of the church in ministry.
  2. Guiding the selection and use of materials in the various agencies and classes of the congregation.
    a. Material that promotes and presents sound Biblical doctrine.
    b. Material that is designed to be an effective teaching tool or aid.
  3. Attending to the spiritual life of the members of the congregation.
    a. Encouraging regular attendance at worship and Bible study, a personal devotional and prayer life, frequent attendance at the Lord's Supper, and the sharing of Jesus with others.
    b. Visiting and encouraging the straying to return to the flock for feeding and growth.
    c. Admonishing and restoring the erring.
    d. Guiding the congregation as Christian discipline is maintained.

  e. Teaching and training the lay ministers as they assist in this spiritual oversight of the flock.

  f. Visiting the sick or dying and those experiencing other crisis situations to minister with the Word and Sacraments.

  g. Counseling with members and others as time allows in order to specifically bring the Word of God to bear on the situations and circumstances of life.

C. The senior pastor shall directly supervise the staff of the congregation:

 1. The professional called workers.

  a. Meeting regularly with the staff for devotions, prayer, sharing, co-ordination, and planning.

  b. Giving encouragement, direction, assignments, and admonitions as are proper.

 2. The salaried (hourly) and volunteer staff.

  a. Directing the work of the administrative assistant, the visitation pastor, the secretaries, and others who may be working in a staff position.

  b. Being directly responsible for the church office and the church secretary.

D. The senior pastor shall be involved in ministry also outside of our congregation by

 1. Serving on boards or committees where his talents, abilities, and interests can help to further the Gospel of the Kingdom. The Board of Lay Ministry will give guidance as to positions that should be accepted.

 2. Leading retreats, conferences, etc. (See II.A.1.a. of this document)

III. Information on Job Requirements

A. The senior pastor should be a strong, devoted man of God who is filled with the Holy Spirit. He should be a man of prayer, an apt Bible student, an able communicator, and always learning (growing in wisdom and stature and in favor with God and man).

B. He should be aware of his strengths as well as his weaknesses and be courageous in leading the flock of the Lord in this place in discipleship and ministry.

C. He should be a man of vision, a compassionate and caring individual with a burning and weeping heart for lost and hurting souls.

D. He should lead the flock by word and personal example.

Job Description: Director of Parish Education and Evangelism (DCE)

I. Job Summary

A. Plan, coordinate, and direct (as necessary) all parish educational programs with the concurrence of the pastor and the Board for Parish Education.

B. Plan and direct an effective evangelism outreach under the supervision of the pastor and the Board of Evangelism.

II. Work Required

A. Principal Duties

 1. Supervise or arrange supervision of all parish educational activities except those specifically delegated to the youth minister. These include:

  a. Pioneer Girls and Brigade Boys

  b. Sunday school and youth Bible classes

  c. Home Bible study program

    d. Special study programs, for example, Christian family classes, etc.

    e. Vacation Bible school

    f. New programs that may be developed and implemented

2. Provide for an accounting and good record keeping of educational activities within the congregation. Assist the Board for Parish Education specifically in this particular task.

3. Plan and provide necessary teacher training opportunities so as to have a qualified cadre of instructors at all levels.

4. Train supervisors—Sunday school superintendent, VBS superintendent, leaders for the Pioneer Girls and Brigade Boys.

5. Continue to develop and train evangelists using the Kennedy method of evangelism training. Help to recruit and emphasize evangelism in all of the activities of the parish.

6. Be an *active evangelist* by making calls regularly during training periods and also as much as possible during other times of the week with special emphasis on follow-up calls and calls generated by our congregational educational programs.

7. Provide for an accounting and good record keeping of the evangelistic outreach opportunities within our congregation. Supervise the keeping of the calling list and the preparation of materials for the nights of evangelism calling.

8. In cooperation with congregational boards and the agencies involved, establish and implement programs to enhance all of the agencies of our congregation as evangelistic outreach arms of the church. This should especially be done in the youth programs and the educational programs.

9. Be a "self-starter" with an eager anticipation to use all gifts and talents in the task before us to the glory and praise of our Lord.

10. Attend meetings of the Board for Parish Education and the Board of Evangelism as a resource person to those boards.

11. Attend meetings of the Church Planning Council as a member of the staff.

12. Work closely with other staff members to coordinate and assist all congregational functions and activities.

B. Subsidiary Activities

    1. Teach classes that are of specific interest, especially adult Bible classes.

    2. Counsel with members and families as time and abilities allow.

    3. Perform special functions that are requested through consultation with the pastor, which are outside the normal functions of the DCE, within limitations imposed by available time.

C. Coordination with Others

    1. The office of director of parish education and evangelism is a derivation of the pastoral office, and consequently the pastor must be kept fully informed of actions and plans of the DCE. To achieve necessary liaison, the DCE will initiate weekly conferences with the pastor (except during their respective vacation periods), sharing with the pastor a report of progress and problems.

    2. Since the Board for Parish Education and the Board of Evangelism are charged with responsibilities to the congregation in their respective areas, the DCE must keep these boards informed of all activities relating to each particular board. Before taking action to change any procedures,

the contemplated action must be cleared with the board or, if between meetings, with the chairman of the board.

3. Through the respective boards the DCE is to help to establish general policies for the functioning of educational and evangelistic programs of the congregation.
4. In any matters concerning doctrine, the DCE should recommend to the boards that the guidance of the pastor be sought before action is taken.
5. If other boards are involved in proposed changes, the DCE should request the necessary liaison with the boards involved to avoid confusion or duplication of effort.

D. Supervision Responsibilities
1. All educational agencies.
2. Assigned counselors and workers with Pioneer Girls and Brigade Boys.
3. All evangelism calling and callers.

III. Information on Job Requirements
A. The DCE should be a graduate of one of our synodical schools and eligible for a call as a full-time staff worker in the church. If such a person is not available, then s/he shall have college-level training and be a member of our church body. Any proposed candidate must exhibit a vibrant and personal faith in Jesus Christ as Lord and Savior and be able to share that faith and hope in an enthusiastic manner.
B. The DCE should be a mature individual (not necessarily in age but in attitude) of stable background, who is capable of
1. Communicating with others orally and in writing;
2. Meeting and dealing with others, whether elders, peers, or juniors;
3. Working independently and acting with perseverance;
4. Developing and presenting technical information relating to the various tasks of the position;
5. Communicating a strong evangelistic desire.

Job Description: Director of Christian Education/Youth Minister

I. Job Summary
A. Develop, implement, and maintain an effective, Christ-centered youth program at our church.
B. Perform such special tasks as counseling and planning retreats, seminars, workshops, etc., for the youth and youth counselors.
C. Achieve the goals for youth that are set forth in the current congregational planning document for growth and evangelism.

II. Work Required
A. Principal Duties
1. Supervise or arrange supervision for the following youth activities (including Christian training and Bible study as well as fellowship):
   a. Regular meetings of junior-high-age member and nonmember youth.
   b. Regular meetings of high-school-age member and nonmember youth.
   c. Activities for college-age youth as feasible and/or requested by the Board of Fellowship.
2. Conduct training sessions at the appropriate level as follows:

      a. Leadership training for adult counselors of junior high and high school youth programs.

      b. Leadership training for adults involved in other youth ministries.

      c. Training for youth leaders within the various youth groups to handle the mechanics of operating the group as a step toward congregational leadership.

      d. Training for youth and youth counselors in evangelism skills through actual scheduled evangelism activities.

  3. Conduct formal instruction in the following areas:

      a. Confirmation class at the seventh grade level.

      b. Sunday Bible study class for high-school-age youth.

      c. Midweek Bible study for high-school-age youth.

      d. Religious education for high-school-age confirmands at the request of the pastor.

      e. Instruction for various age levels of youth and adult counselors in the principles of effective youth evangelism.

  4. Conduct visitations of youth in the congregation and of prospective members, with their families, in their homes. This shall be considered an ongoing task of the highest priority.

  5. Attend meetings of the Board of Youth Ministry and serve as an adviser and resource person to that body.

  6. Attend meetings of the Church Planning Council as a member of the staff.

  7. Work closely with the DCE/Evangelism and the superintendent of the Sunday school to coordinate youth and Sunday school activities whenever appropriate.

 B. Subsidiary Activities

  1. Perform professional counseling with youth who are not directly under the pastor's care as a need is discerned during day-to-day contact within following areas:

      a. Personal problems due to home background or environment.

      b. Career decisions common to high school age youth.

      c. Spiritual counseling.

  2. Perform special functions that are requested through consultation with the pastor, which are outside the normal functions of the DCE/Youth Minister.

 C. Coordination with Others

  1. The office of DCE/Youth Minister derives from the pastoral office, and consequently the pastor must be kept fully informed. To achieve the necessary liaison, the DCE/Youth Minister will initiate weekly conferences with the pastor (except during their respective vacation periods), sharing with the pastor a report of progress and problems.

  2. Since the Board of Youth Ministry is responsible to the congregation for an effective youth program, the DCE/Youth Minister must keep that body fully informed of all activities. Before taking action to change any procedures, the contemplated action must be cleared with the board or, if between meetings, with the chairman of the board.

III. Information on Job Requirements

 A. The DCE/Youth Minister should be a graduate of one of our synodical schools and eligible for a call as a full-time staff worker in the church. If such a person is not available, then s/he shall have college-level training and be a member of our church body. Any proposed candidate must exhibit a vibrant and personal faith in Jesus Christ as Lord and Savior and be able to share that faith and hope in an enthusiastic manner.

B. The DCE/Youth Minister should be a mature individual (not necessarily in age but in attitude) of stable background, who is capable of
   1. Communicating with others orally and in writing;
   2. Meeting and dealing with others, whether elders, peers, or juniors;
   3. Working independently and acting with perseverance;
   4. Developing and presenting technical information relating to the various tasks of the position;
   4. Communicating a strong evangelistic desire.

Parish School

(The following sample illustrates a job description for a principal and assistant principal of a parish school with an enrollment of 300 students.)

Job Description: Principal and Assistant Principal

The Board for Parochial Education delegates to the principal and the assistant principal the responsibility for the daily operation of the school. The school program should be administered and supervised in accord with the policies adopted by the board.

I. Qualifications
   A. A master's degree or higher, with an emphasis in elementary education administration.
   B. A valid state certificate to practice as an elementary principal.
   C. At least four years of successful experience as a classroom teacher.
   D. Membership in this congregation.
   E. Such alternatives to the above qualifications as the board may find appropriate and acceptable.

II. Accountability
   The principal and assistant principal are accountable to the congregation through its Board for Parochial Education.

III. Supervision
   A. All personnel serving in the school.
   B. Other resource and service personnel while they are functioning in the school, including secretary, kitchen workers, bus drivers, and custodian.

IV. Responsibilities
   A. Principal
      1. Participates in parish leadership by working cooperatively with pastors and Board of Directors.
      2. Works with pastors to maintain the integral role of the school in the mission and ministry of the church.
      3. Meets regularly with the pastors to participate in unified parish planning.
      4. Meets regularly with the pastors to plan their participation in school activities.
      5. Prepares reports required by local, state, national, and District officials and keeps current files of reports.
      6. Promotes the school and encourages parents to enroll their children in the school through a program of soul accounting.

7. Sends school news to parents regularly. Prepares annual school handbook, faculty handbook, etc.
8. Enrolls students in accordance with policies established by the Board for Parochial Education.
9. Orders and purchases all school materials and equipment and keeps a complete inventory of these materials and equipment.
10. Collects all monies and maintains an accurate financial record.
11. Prepares the board agenda in consultation with the chairperson and communicates the decisions of the board to teachers, students, and parents.
12. Advises the congregation on school finance and the school calendar.
13. Arranges regular and purposeful meetings of teachers and, as needed, of the nonteaching staff.
14. Uses the available media to provide publicity about the school to the community.
15. Advises and coordinates the activities of the parent-teacher association through the faculty representative.
16. Appoints delegates or representatives to organizations and committees.
17. Works with the superintendent of our denomination's schools in this city in carrying out busing, special education, music, and other cooperative programs.
18. Meets monthly with the superintendent and principals of sister schools of this city.
19. Coordinates any public school services available to our students and staff.

B. Assistant Principal
1. Develops and improves the curriculum and provides for teacher and parent involvement in curriculum study, construction, and revision.
2. Promotes the professional growth of the staff.
3. Supervises the instructional program of the school so that the philosophy and curricular objectives are fulfilled.
4. Develops and carries out a program of evaluation of the teaching personnel.
5. Maintains the standard of behavior established for the school and works with the teachers and staff to provide for uniform application of regulations.
6. Provides an effective guidance program.
7. Supervises custodians in the safety, cleaning, and good maintenance of all facilities and reports any personnel problems to the Board of Properties.

C. Principal and Assistant Principal Jointly
1. Help the board develop policies and implement the adopted policies.
2. Represent the needs of the staff before the board.
3. Play a leading role in securing qualified personnel for the school and orient new staff members.
4. Assign extra duties and orient new personnel to those special duties.
5. Are concerned about the progress of each child in the school and seek to establish good rapport with the students through openness with them and fair treatment in handling problems that arise.

6. Supervise school time schedules for coordination and smooth operation of the instructional program.
7. Have released time from teaching responsibility, the amount to be determined each year mutually among the principals and the board.
8. Work with the Board of Properties for the safety and good maintenance of all facilities.

V. Terms of Employment
The principal and assistant principal have continuous employment with four weeks of annual vacation.

VI. Salary
The Board of Directors through its appointed committee annually evaluates salaries and recommends changes.

VII. Evaluation
The performance of these offices will be evaluated annually by the Board for Parochial Education.

(The following sample illustrates the job description of a teacher in a parish school with an enrollment of 250 students.)

Job Description: Elementary Christian Day School Teacher

A. Accountability
The teacher is a minister of our congregation. S/he works cooperatively as a team member with all other personnel of the school and church. The teacher's supervisor is the principal of the school, who receives the teacher's school-related reports, questions, and concerns. The teacher will meet with the principal and senior pastor each June in order to review the nonschool assignments in the congregation's ministry and to recommend jointly any changes to the boards responsible for those ministries for the year ahead. Accountability is to the chairperson of those boards.

B. Personal Qualifications
The teacher associates closely with God through prayer, study of the Scriptures, and regular church and Communion attendance. S/he gives ample evidence of a life-style that reflects a dynamic relationship with Christ. The teacher is open-minded and tolerant and has a happy and positive outlook on life. S/he is sensitive to the needs of others, cares about the feelings of others, shows Christian concern for all, maintains confidences, and is respectful of others. S/he uses correct language and written forms. S/he is tactful, warm, and courteous and is an effective listener. The physical and emotional health of the teacher is good, and s/he is poised, punctual, and enthusiastic. The teacher is able to articulate clearly the objectives of our Christian school and evidences a love for teaching children. S/he makes a good appearance in terms of dress and style and attends and participates in church and community activities.

C. Professional Qualifications
The teacher holds teaching ministry certification from our national church body or has indicated intent to meet the requirements to do so. S/he holds the minimum of a bachelor's degree in education. The teacher has been certified by the state department of education or will soon be able to receive such certification. S/he understands and supports the congregation's program of education for all grade levels.

D. The Teaching Position
This position assigns the teacher to instruct the fourth grade, which will have approximately 25 students in a self-contained classroom. The teacher will be responsible for teaching all the fourth grade subjects except physical education, which will be taught four days a week by the fifth grade teacher. The fourth grade teacher will in turn instruct two periods of fifth grade art and two of fifth grade music each week.

E. Classroom Responsibilities
The following are the general daily expectations for the operation and climate of the teacher's classroom:
   1. Brief, meaningful worship opens and closes each day.
   2. Instruction is related to the school's Christian objectives.
   3. The children are effectively and fairly controlled. Discipline is applied according to Christian methods that use the Law and Gospel appropriately and well.
   4. The room is neat and clean. It presents an enjoyable, learning-oriented environment for children.
   5. Basic planning is done in each subject for the year, and goals are set each quarter in order to cover the material in the school's curriculum for the year.
   6. A daily schedule is used that meets the school's time allotments and ties in smoothly with the other classrooms.
   7. A lesson plan book is used to briefly describe and organize daily instruction, and written lesson outlines are prepared daily for all subjects.
   8. Communication is clear and effective. Children are being constantly reinforced, both verbally and nonverbally, in positive ways.
   9. Various teaching procedures, audio-visual aids, and motivational techniques are in regular use.
   10. Children's desks are arranged for effective learning and behavior, and a seating chart is kept.
   11. Children's learning progress is monitored through effective evaluation and testing. Learning activities and assignments are adjusted as much as possible in order to provide for individual differences. Both enrichment and remedial activities are in regular use. The school's standardized tests are administered and used.
   12. Records of attendance and achievement are kept for each student.

F. Other School Responsibilities
In order to maintain an effective overall school program, the teaching position involves the following additional items:
   1. Visiting the homes of all the fourth graders' parents in August before school begins.
   2. Attending all faculty meetings, which will include a preschool workshop in August and postschool meetings in June.
   3. Arriving at school by 7:50 a.m., attending daily faculty devotions at 7:55 a.m., and leaving school no earlier than 3:55 p.m.
   4. Preparing quarterly report cards for parents and meeting with all parents on the two designated annual conference days.
   5. Attending all teacher conferences.
   6. Serving as the coach of the girls' volleyball team for 10 weeks each fall.

This includes three time periods each week—generally two practices and one game.

7. Directing the annual Kindergarten-Grade 4 musical/operetta, which is held in May.
8. Visiting all the congregation's nonschool parents of fourth graders during June in order to discuss their program of Christian nurture and potential use of the school.

G. Other Parish Responsibilities
1. Present a children's message for Sunday worship services once each half year.
2. Serve as a member of the Board for Adult Nurture.
3. Teach the sixth grade Sunday school class from September through January.
4. Conduct a six-week Sunday school teachers course in March and April in even-numbered years.
5. Teach the third grade of the annual two-week vacation church school.

H. Terms of Service
As a member of our congregation's professional ministry staff, the teacher receives a call into our service. S/he accepts a tenured, full-time position. While tenure is granted already at the time of acceptance of the call, it is given with the understanding that the teacher will not only strive for excellence in the initial year but also annually pursue the professional and personal growth that will assure continued excellence. Every April a thorough evaluation of the teacher's ministry will be made by the principal and the senior pastor in order to assist the teacher in maintaining a high caliber of service. Personal integrity, job satisfaction, and job performance will be the basic elements of this evaluation.

Support Staff

(The following sample illustrates a job description for a church secretary in a mid-size congregation.)

Job Description: Parish Office Secretary

The parish secretary shall work principally under the pastor(s) and shall be responsible for the following:

1. Serving as the main receptionist of the church.
2. Answering the telephone and scheduling all appointments, interviews, calls, etc., for the pastor(s).
3. Receiving calls concerning the scheduling of weddings, baptisms, funerals, etc., and scheduling these events in consultation with the pastor(s).
4. Notifying the pastor(s) and other concerned persons of problems, illness, hospitalization, death, etc.
5. Typing all forms, records, and correspondence for the pastor(s).
6. Keeping all official records of the congregation up-to-date: baptisms, confirmations, weddings, funerals, transfers, Communion records.
7. Helping the financial secretary with various duties: issuing church envelopes to new members, recording envelope numbers and pledge amounts, typing and distributing financial record forms each year for

the recording secretaries, preparing additional forms when new members transfer in.

8. Preparing the baptismal, membership, confirmation, and wedding (county and church) certificates and seeing that they are properly signed by the pastor(s).
9. Directing all requests for membership changes to the pastor(s).
10. Typing and mailing all transfers and seeing that they are properly signed.
11. Mailing letters and packages and purchasing stamps and other petty cash items.
12. Handling the church office petty cash fund, keeping all records and receipts for expenditures, and doing the bookkeeping necessary to keep the checkbook in balance and in agreement with bank statements.
13. Dispatching promptly all incoming mail to the recipient and mailing all outgoing mail.
14. Preparing and maintaining an annual and monthly schedule of events.
15. Keeping the master activities calendar and wedding calendar current.
16. Preparing lists of needed office supplies and ordering them through proper channels.
17. Gathering information, typing the masters, proofreading, and printing the church bulletins for each Sunday.
18. Advising members of church auxiliary organizations who have special printing projects on the preparation of masters, the type of paper to use, probable length of time for preparation, etc.
19. Preparing statements of charges for special printing work done for outside organizations (requires familiarity with the cost of all supplies used in reproduction work).
20. Cleaning and ordering supplies for the photocopy machine.
21. Operating dictating equipment.
22. Maintaining confidentiality.
23. Organizing volunteer workers.
24. Performing all other tasks that may arise at the request of the pastor(s).

Appendix B
Sample Table
of Contents—
Parish Personnel
Policy Handbook

A. Introduction to Handbook
   1. "Clear Expectations"
   2. Personnel Committee
   3. Accountability to Parish Boards
B. Job Descriptions
   JD-1 Statement of Accountability
   JD-2 List of Personal Qualifications
   JD-3 List of Professional Qualifications
   JD-4 Position Summary
   JD-5 List of Responsibilities
   JD-6 Terms of Service
C. Employment Policies
   EP-1 General Statement
   EP-2 Regarding Equal Opportunity/Church Restrictions
   EP-3 Selection and Appointment
      a. Procedures for Calling or Contracting Pastors, Teachers, and Other Ministers
      b. Procedures for Hiring Auxiliary Staff
   EP-4 Classification of Employees
   EP-5 Tenure for Ministry Staff
   EP-6 Trial or Probationary Period for Auxiliary Staff
   EP-7 Anniversary Date
D. Wage and Salary Policies
   WS-1 Establishing Wages and Salaries
      a. Salary Schedule for Ministry Staff
      b. Wages for Auxiliary Staff Positions

Appendix C
Aids for Assisting Church Staff Teams in Identifying Areas for Team Ministry Growth and Development

1. Developing Your Team Ministry

A. Getting Started
   1. Identify three of your strengths as a team member:

   _____

   _____

   _____

   2. Identify three of your weaknesses as a team member:

   _____

   _____

   _____

3. Identify three characteristics of someone you would consider to be the "perfect" staff person with whom to work:

_____

_____

_____

4. Identify five "ideal principles" for an effective team ministry relationship (i.e., open communication, empathy, recognition, etc.):

_____

_____

_____

_____

_____

5. Suppose you accept a call to a congregation that has been served previously by a multiple staff. What three key questions would you ask regarding team ministry?

_____

_____

_____

B. Continuum
   For team ministry to be effective, the following components are needed:

   1. A clear definition of our roles/functions/responsibilities

   |⎯⎯⎯⎯|⎯⎯⎯⎯|⎯⎯⎯⎯|⎯⎯⎯⎯|⎯⎯⎯⎯|⎯⎯⎯⎯|⎯⎯⎯⎯|⎯⎯⎯⎯|
   Strongly agree   Neutral   Strongly disagree

   2. Clearly defined goals for one's own personal ministry

   |⎯⎯⎯⎯|⎯⎯⎯⎯|⎯⎯⎯⎯|⎯⎯⎯⎯|⎯⎯⎯⎯|⎯⎯⎯⎯|⎯⎯⎯⎯|⎯⎯⎯⎯|
   Strongly agree   Neutral   Strongly disagree

   3. Openness and trust in the relationship

   |⎯⎯⎯⎯|⎯⎯⎯⎯|⎯⎯⎯⎯|⎯⎯⎯⎯|⎯⎯⎯⎯|⎯⎯⎯⎯|⎯⎯⎯⎯|⎯⎯⎯⎯|
   Strongly agree   Neutral   Strongly disagree

   4. An established time for staff meetings

   |⎯⎯⎯⎯|⎯⎯⎯⎯|⎯⎯⎯⎯|⎯⎯⎯⎯|⎯⎯⎯⎯|⎯⎯⎯⎯|⎯⎯⎯⎯|⎯⎯⎯⎯|
   Strongly agree   Neutral   Strongly disagree

5. Support for the activities of all staff members within the congregation

|_____|_____|_____|_____|_____|_____|_____|_____|_____|_____|
Strongly agree   Neutral   Strongly disagree

6. Accessibility to one another

|_____|_____|_____|_____|_____|_____|_____|_____|_____|_____|
Strongly agree   Neutral   Strongly disagree

7. Spending time together on a social basis

|_____|_____|_____|_____|_____|_____|_____|_____|_____|_____|
Strongly agree   Neutral   Strongly disagree

8. Equal salaries in proportion to years of experience

|_____|_____|_____|_____|_____|_____|_____|_____|_____|_____|
Strongly agree   Neutral   Strongly disagree

9. Each staff member to be involved in the total parish ministry

|_____|_____|_____|_____|_____|_____|_____|_____|_____|_____|
Strongly agree   Neutral   Strongly disagree

10. All staff members to be responsible to the pastor (senior pastor if there is more than one pastor)

|_____|_____|_____|_____|_____|_____|_____|_____|_____|_____|
Strongly agree   Neutral   Strongly disagree

11. Total staff involved in worship services

|_____|_____|_____|_____|_____|_____|_____|_____|_____|_____|
Strongly agree   Neutral   Strongly disagree

12. Clarity about who finally "calls the shots"

|_____|_____|_____|_____|_____|_____|_____|_____|_____|_____|
Strongly agree   Neutral   Strongly disagree

13. Clear indication of how each staff member's work is to be evaluated

|_____|_____|_____|_____|_____|_____|_____|_____|_____|_____|
Strongly agree   Neutral   Strongly disagree

14. Respect for personal and professional confidences

|_____|_____|_____|_____|_____|_____|_____|_____|_____|_____|
Strongly agree   Neutral   Strongly disagree

15. Affirmation and support from and for each other

|_____|_____|_____|_____|_____|_____|_____|_____|_____|_____|
Strongly agree   Neutral   Strongly disagree

16. Acceptance of disagreements on procedures, activities, programs, etc.

|_____|_____|_____|_____|_____|_____|_____|_____|_____|_____|
Strongly agree   Neutral   Strongly disagree

17. Acknowledgment of mistakes and failures

Strongly agree — Neutral — Strongly disagree

18. Decisions by consensus

Strongly agree — Neutral — Strongly disagree

19. Close ties with each other's families

Strongly agree — Neutral — Strongly disagree

20. A day off for each staff member

Strongly agree — Neutral — Strongly disagree

21. Freedom to be "creative"

Strongly agree — Neutral — Strongly disagree

22. Equal recognition on church bulletins, signs, directory, etc.

Strongly agree — Neutral — Strongly disagree

23. Recognition that all are ministers of the Gospel, differing only in function and gifts

Strongly agree — Neutral — Strongly disagree

24. Understanding and consensus about staff member accountability

Strongly agree — Neutral — Strongly disagree

C. Contract Making

What specific things can I do to develop a more positive and effective team ministry back home?

_____

_____

(Used by permission of LeRoy R. Wilke, assistant professor and coordinator of the Director of Christian Education Program at Concordia College, St. Paul, MN.)

2. Behavior Description Questionnaire

A. Relations with Others

This form is designed to help you describe your current and preferred ways of relating to others.

For each of the statements below, draw a line through the number that best describes your current behavior. Next, circle the number that best expresses what you would like your behavior to be.

1. Ability to listen to others in an understanding way.

not at all able   1 : 2 : 3 : 4 : 5 : 6 : 7 : 8 : 9   completely able

2. Willingness to discuss feelings with others.

completely unwilling   1 : 2 : 3 : 4 : 5 : 6 : 7 : 8 : 9   completely willing

3. Awareness of the feelings of others.

completely unaware   1 : 2 : 3 : 4 : 5 : 6 : 7 : 8 : 9   completely aware

4. Understanding why I do what I do.

no understanding at all   1 : 2 : 3 : 4 : 5 : 6 : 7 : 8 : 9   complete understanding

5. Reactions to conflict and antagonism.

uncomfortable with   1 : 2 : 3 : 4 : 5 : 6 : 7 : 8 : 9   tolerant

6. Reactions to expressions of affection and warmth among others.

uncomfortable   1 : 2 : 3 : 4 : 5 : 6 : 7 : 8 : 9   accepting

7. Reactions to comments about my behavior from others.

rejecting   1 : 2 : 3 : 4 : 5 : 6 : 7 : 8 : 9   welcome

8. Willingness to trust others.

completely unwilling   1 : 2 : 3 : 4 : 5 : 6 : 7 : 8 : 9   completely willing

9. Ability to influence others.

no ability at all   1 : 2 : 3 : 4 : 5 : 6 : 7 : 8 : 9   completely able

B. Learning, Problem-Solving Style

1. Tendency to seek out learning opportunities.

content to wait   1 : 2 : 3 : 4 : 5 : 6 : 7 : 8 : 9   always searching

2. Breadth of focus.

intensive narrow focus   1 : 2 : 3 : 4 : 5 : 6 : 7 : 8 : 9   extensive wide search for solutions and understanding

3. Speed of decision.

defer judgment as long as possible   1 : 2 : 3 : 4 : 5 : 6 : 7 : 8 : 9   decide as quickly as possible

4. Objective or intuitive approach to problems.

rely *exclusively* on *feelings*, not facts   1 : 2 : 3 : 4 : 5 : 6 : 7 : 8 : 9   rely exclusively on *facts*, not feelings

5. Impulsiveness.

speak before I think   1 : 2 : 3 : 4 : 5 : 6 : 7 : 8 : 9   think before I speak

6. Imitation or independent problem solving.

learn exclusively from others   1 : 2 : 3 : 4 : 5 : 6 : 7 : 8 : 9   always solve problems for myself

7. Persistence.

give up too quickly on tough problems   1 : 2 : 3 : 4 : 5 : 6 : 7 : 8 : 9   never give up

8. Problem identification.

never see myself as part of the problem   1 : 2 : 3 : 4 : 5 : 6 : 7 : 8 : 9   always see myself as a major part of the problem

9. Internal-external focus.

completely controlled by my environment   1 : 2 : 3 : 4 : 5 : 6 : 7 : 8 : 9   completely controlled by my inner thoughts and feelings

C. Managerial Style

1. Risk-taking under uncertainty.

extremely cautious   1 : 2 : 3 : 4 : 5 : 6 : 7 : 8 : 9   extremely adventuresome

2. Attention to detail.

concentrate on details   1 : 2 : 3 : 4 : 5 : 6 : 7 : 8 : 9   always ignore details, leave to others

3. Concern for welfare of subordinates.

no concern at all   1 : 2 : 3 : 4 : 5 : 6 : 7 : 8 : 9   complete concern

4. Relationship to higher authority.

always lean on authority   1 : 2 : 3 : 4 : 5 : 6 : 7 : 8 : 9   always rebel against authority

5. Delegation.

prefer to let others solve problems   1 : 2 : 3 : 4 : 5 : 6 : 7 : 8 : 9   prefer to solve problems myself

6. Time perspective.

short-run maximizer   1 : 2 : 3 : 4 : 5 : 6 : 7 : 8 : 9   always consider the long-range view

7. Individual or group decisions.

prefer individual decisions   1 : 2 : 3 : 4 : 5 : 6 : 7 : 8 : 9   prefer group decisions

8. Concern for rules.

| disregard whenever they get in the way | 1 : 2 : 3 : 4 : 5 : 6 : 7 : 8 : 9 | obey completely |

9. Influence style.

| rely on "politicking," alliances, and bargaining | 1 : 2 : 3 : 4 : 5 : 6 : 7 : 8 : 9 | rely on open communication and trust |

10. Use of authority in getting work done.

| rely on my position | 1 : 2 : 3 : 4 : 5 : 6 : 7 : 8 : 9 | rely on persuasion and/or personality |

11. Task concerns.

| concerned exclusively with budgets, costs, getting the job done | 1 : 2 : 3 : 4 : 5 : 6 : 7 : 8 : 9 | concerned exclusively with maintaining good working relations |

12. Relationship with peers.

| highly cooperative | 1 : 2 : 3 : 4 : 5 : 6 : 7 : 8 : 9 | highly competitive |

D. Team Development Scale

1. Degree of mutual trust.

| high suspicion | 1 : 2 : 3 : 4 : 5 : 6 : 7 : 8 : 9 | high trust |

2. Communications.

| guarded, cautious | 1 : 2 : 3 : 4 : 5 : 6 : 7 : 8 : 9 | open, authentic |

3. Degree of mutual support.

| totally interested in self | 1 : 2 : 3 : 4 : 5 : 6 : 7 : 8 : 9 | genuine concern for each other |

4. Team objectives.

| not understood | 1 : 2 : 3 : 4 : 5 : 6 : 7 : 8 : 9 | clearly understood |

5. Handling conflicts within the team.

| denial, avoidance, suppression, or compromise | 1 : 2 : 3 : 4 : 5 : 6 : 7 : 8 : 9 | acceptance and "working through" conflicts |

6. Utilization of member resources.

| competencies used by team | 1 : 2 : 3 : 4 : 5 : 6 : 7 : 8 : 9 | competencies not used |

7. Control methods.

| control is imposed | 1 : 2 : 3 : 4 : 5 : 6 : 7 : 8 : 9 | control from within |

8. Organizational environment.

| restrictive, pressure for conformity | 1 : 2 : 3 : 4 : 5 : 6 : 7 : 8 : 9 | free, supportive, respect for differences |

Bibliography

Books

Bonhoeffer, Dietrich. *Life Together*. Ed. and tr. John W. Doberstein. New York: Harper and Row Publishers, 1954.

Douglas, Stephen B., Bruce E. Cook, and Howard G. Hendricks. *The Ministry of Management*. San Bernardino, Calif.: Campus Crusade for Christ International, 1981.

Engstrom, Ted W. *The Making of a Christian Leader*. Grand Rapids, Mich.: Zondervan, 1976.

Hoover, David W., and Roger W. Leenerts. *Enlightened with His Gifts*. St. Louis: Lutheran Growth, 1979.

Lair, Jess. *I Ain't Much Baby--but I'm All I've Got*. New York: Fawcett Crest Books, 1972.

Schaller, Lyle E. *The Multiple Staff and the Larger Church*. Nashville: Abingdon, 1980.

Tubesing, Donald A., and Nancy Loving Tubesing. *The Caring Question*. Minneapolis: Augsburg Publishing House, 1983.

Wagner, C. Peter. *Your Spiritual Gifts Can Help You Grow*. Glendale, Calif.: Regal Books Division, G/L Publications, 1979.

Booklet

Reflections on Team Ministry. River Forest, Ill.: Lutheran Education Association, 1984 (25 pages).

Periodicals

Engstrom, Ted W., and Edward R. Dayton, eds. "Teamwork," *Christian Leadership Letter*. June 1983.

Gundermann, Vernon D. " 'Teaming'," *Lutheran Education* 118 (March-April 1983): 212—17.

Hunter, Kent R. "A Model for Middle Staff Management," *Leadership* 2, no. 3 (Summer 1981): 99—107.

Jacobsen, Wayne L. "Caught in the Middle," *Leadership* 1, no. 2 (Spring 1980): 83—90.

Lauterbach, Kermit R. "The Hazards of Being an Associate Minister," *Issues in Christian Education* 10, no. 1 (Fall 1975): 14—17.

Martin, Gilbert R. "Testing Staff Relationships in the High Sierras," *Leadership* 2, no. 2 (Spring 1981): 79—86.

Muck, Terry. "How I Motivate My Staff," *Leadership* 1, no. 3 (Summer 1980): 81—84.

Schoedel, Walter M. "Pastor-Principal-Teacher Relationships: A More Excellent Way," *Lutheran Education* 116 (March-April 1981): 199—203.

Schoedel, Walter M. "The Hazards of Being Chief Shepherd," *Issues in Christian Education* 10, no. 1 (Fall 1975): 10—13.

Shawchuck, Norman. "A Candid Letter to Senior Pastors," *Leadership* 1, no. 2 (Summer 1980): 85—87.

Smith, Fred. "Building the Church Staff," *Leadership* 3, no. 4 (Fall 1982): 99—104.

Manuals

Aid Association for Lutherans. *Project SERVE: Lutheran Schools.* Operations Manual. Appleton, Wis., 1982.

Myers Briggs Type Indicator. Palo Alto, Calif.: Consulting Psychologists Press, Inc., 1976

The Personal Profile System. Performax Systems International, Inc., 1977.